Other Books by Georgia S. McDade

Outside the Cave 1

Outside the Cave 2

Outside the Cave 3

Outside the Cave 4

Travel Tips for Dream Trips

Observations and Revelations

A Collection of Stories, Sketches, and Essays

by

Georgia S. McDade, Ph. D.

Book & Cover Design by Vladimir Verano, Vertvolta design

www.vertvoltapress.com

Contact the author:

gsmcdade@msn.com

First Edition

ISBN: 978-0-9821872-2-7

This book is dedicated to the memory of

Georgia Harvey Allen Stewart,

my beloved mother and number one fan.

Acknowledgements

Thanks to Lola E. Peters for computer expertise, Kathya Alexander and Randee Eddins for suggestions on "Ain't 'm Livin'?" Carolyn Simonson for reading the manuscript, and Frank Weihs for editing.

Thanks to Richard Curtner for permission to use his word collage *Open Book* on the cover.

Thanks to Vladimir Verano for the layout and patience.

Thanks also to everyone who shared experiences with me.

A special thanks to persons who have heard the stories and asked for a copy!

Only within the past few months has it dawned on me that I tell a story—verbal or written—after the event, sometimes ages after the event. I never sit and say I'm going to tell a story. Through observation I concluded a truth, perhaps a mere kernel of a truth but a truth nevertheless. I may have seen the truth many times; I may have had the truth revealed to me; I may have witnessed an epiphany. I do not always agree or like or subscribe to the truths. The truths may have origins of various kinds: personal experience; someone else's experience; a movie; a literary vehicle; any action or interaction with persons and/or animals. What I know is that I saw and then took the time to write, sometimes almost immediately, other times years later.

Another of my realizations is much, much older. I live by rules, codes. I do not know when I realized this truth, but during my decades of teaching adults I soon realized that all of us have certain rules that govern our actions. These rules may be ever so obvious to us and others; they may be invisible to us and others. The first day of a college humanities class I would ask students to make a list of rules they live by. Quarter after quarter I saw the same behavior: some students began writing immediately; others required more time; some could come up with only one rule; others could come up with ten or twelve rules; some had to be prompted—what did your mom or dad ALWAYS tell you? At least one person always proclaimed, "I live by no rules." I always responded the same: "That is a rule."

Throughout the quarter there were students who would refer to something they had written that first day. Granted, some of us may add or delete codes, but generally it seems we humans have a core of values, some values obvious, other values not. We can change, for the good and for the bad, particularly if there is a traumatic happening in our lives. But generally, I have come to believe that we act or don't act according to our rules. The sooner we learn that some person's rules are diametrically opposite to ours, the easier we can negotiate life.

This first-day assignment in literature and humanities classes required students to write the "Codes I Live By (Usually)." I too wrote.

Codes I Live By (Usually)

1. *I treat people the way I want to be treated. (Matthew 7:12, Luke 6:31)*
2. *I can adapt, migrate, or die in any situation.*
3. *Life is a struggle.*
4. *I am what has happened to me, but I am also what has not happened to me.*
5. *I don't always learn the same lessons as others do from the same examples.*
6. *I can place the people in the world in four groups: those who don't know I exist (most); those who are indifferent to my existence; those who wish me ill; those who wish me well.*
7. *Sometimes there is absolutely nothing I can do to change a situation regardless of my desire, sincerity, skills, concern, involvement, resources, or whatever.*

8. *Jesus did not convert everybody; there were those who came in contact with Him and did not believe.*

9. *There is very little equality in the world.*

10. *Life is not fair.*

11. *The situation can always get worse. ("The worst is not so long as we can say, 'This is the worst.'" (King Lear IV i 28)*

12. *I give without expecting thanks.*

13. *I pass a kindness to someone whenever I can.*

14. *Living requires risks.*

15. *I can never see the whole picture; I have to act on what I know.*

16. *There is nothing everyone knows.*

17. *Being right, sincere, honest, kind, understanding does not necessarily make others see me as right, sincere, honest, kind, understanding.*

18. *Kermit—the green frog— and the blind Ray Charles sing "It is not easy being green": I say it is not easy being.*

19. *I don't ask others to do what I haven't done, don't do, won't do.*

20. *I may never learn what some want me to learn when they want me to learn it and how they want me to learn it.*

21. *Sincerely wanting the best for someone doesn't mean that it is the best OR that the person wants it.*

22. *"O, reason not the need. Our basest beggars are in the poorest thing superfluous." (King Lear IV ii 264-265)*

23. *Change is inevitable; how I respond to it makes all the difference.*

All but five of the above were written in one period of less than fifteen minutes. By the time I was ready to type this—about three weeks later—I wanted to add other statements. But I thought it only fair not to change the list. These statements are not necessarily listed in order of importance. But they govern my actions in varying degrees. I face—and overcome—many challenges because these statements provide guidelines for me.

Agree! Disagree! Cite examples! Cite examples to the contrary!

See what happens when all of the "I's" are replaced with "we's."

See what happens when all of the "I's" are replaced with "you's."

Years later the list continues to be accurate. There are a few more rules I would like to add, but I'll add only one: "You may set your standards as high as you want, and you can live up to your standards. But you should not expect others to live up to your standards, and you certainly should not be upset with them when they don't." The statement was to me, from my mother, when I was about eight or possibly younger. I had forgotten this statement until my brother reminded me of it about two years ago. In the midst of us seven siblings in four states sporadically listing what our mother used to say, my brother revealed this one. Of course, I remembered after his reminder! As I thought about the disagreements I have had over the years, especially the major ones, an epiphany appeared: at the root of the differences was always a difference in standards.

I can see how this as well as the twenty-three "codes" above, serve, to varying degrees, to determine what I record in stories. What I hope most is that your reading of the stories will provide observations, revelations, and/or epiphanies.

Georgia S. McDade, Ph. D.

2/26/15

Contents

Ain't 'm Livin'?

When Daddy was six, his father was killed, killed the day after he he had gambled his way to victory over a white man. By the time Daddy was eight, he had to quit school so he could help Grandma take care of his younger siblings. By the time I was eight, I knew not to mention anything about school if money was involved. Daddy said, "I didn't go no further than the third grade. Look at me. You don't need to go to school." As a youngster I always had the feeling that he felt cheated but he didn't think he was supposed to feel that way, so he never said anything good about going to school.

I do not know when he met M'Dear, only that he was a handsome man who dated a number of women, all of whom seemed to have found him attractive. I do not know when they married. But I do know he was twenty-nine when my oldest sister was born. I grew up listening to stories about how he adored this daughter, how he took her everywhere with him. I never doubted the stories because although there are eight of us, she is the only one of us who appears in a photograph with him.

There was a time when Daddy, M'Dear, and my sister lived in the country. Daddy was a sharecropper. I remember stories of how Mr. Beal beat so many people out of their money. The people worked and worked, always thinking this was their last year on the farm. They would be ready to go. Then Mr. Beal would pay them. But then he would show them how they signed for this and that and that and this. Soon any fool could see that a family would have to work harder and at least another year to get out of Mr. Beal's debt. I do not know how long it took Daddy to escape, but he did. And he often talked about how other families would die working for Mr. Beal. Years later I recall how he protested vehemently when one of my friends said she knew I had grown up on a farm. With pride he said, "Not her! She don't know nothin' 'bout no farm!"

I know he went to the army—he spent time in Seattle. But he was discharged early because he had a medical disability. My sister says it was asthma.

He came back to Monroe where he worked during the day and went to vocational school at night. He was like many veterans who went to school on the G.I. Bill. I remember how M'Dear, my brother, aunt, and I would walk to the school at night and ride home with him. Long after he stopped attending school I recall how we always referred to the building as the place where Daddy went to school. I have no idea what he was studying.

His job was driving a truck for several grocery companies—Salley, Drew. I do not remember him ever making over forty dollars a week. For a time he worked for the City. I still remember what he bought for grocery every week: twenty-five pounds of Gold Medal flour, twenty-five pounds of meal, lard, bacon, Godchaux sugar, chicken, Maxwell House coffee, Coca-Cola, soap, bananas, sometimes oranges. Anything else, M'Dear bought.

He always had a car. The '46 Chevrolet is the first one I remember. There were several other cars, but he never owned one as long as he owned that one. Not one was new. But he did manage to get the cutest little green station wagon, a Pontiac, an almost new car. He kept it so clean. He never said so, but I always knew he was proud of it. He must have had it about a year.

I do not know what my brother did—he was often in trouble. He never did anything seriously bad, but he did enough to keep

M'Dear trying to get him out of trouble. Somehow Daddy managed not to be involved. He fussed and cussed, but that was it. Then my brother did something serious. Somebody filed a suit. One day some men came to take the little green car. Daddy had never had my sympathy as he had it that time. He did not fuss or cuss. He just sat on the porch, dejected. He looked so beaten. It was as if he had absolutely no fight. He soon got another car, older, not nearly so neat. I do not remember what it was, but it was never as clean as the little green Pontiac.

Shortly afterward, I went to college. Since my mom wrote me two letters a day—one came in the morning mail, and one came in the afternoon mail—I usually knew what Daddy was doing. He still went fishing, most of the time by himself. He still hunted, sometimes with two or three friends, but most of the time by himself. Many days he would go hunting, kill the limit, return home, go back, and kill the limit again. Whenever any of us complained that we wanted meat, he would tell us that we had meat: squirrel and rabbit. Not very much seemed to change. It was only years later that a sister assured me that life was worse after I left. Daddy bought grocery less, gave them dinner money (.15) for school less often, fussed and cussed more.

He had never gotten along with any of the neighbors. He had a name for everybody, especially the women. There was Gorilla, Monkey, Elephant Ass, and so forth. When I think about the fact that he never called these people by their names and we always knew whom he was talking about but never divulged these names, I smile. He and one man, Mr. Willie, fussed more than anybody on the street. I think the man's dog—Black Gal—was the source of much of the friction. Daddy tried to poison her on more than one occasion—at least he threatened to. One day Daddy was clearing the ditch on city property in front of our door. When it rained, the water in the ditch would often back up and become stagnant. M'Dear said Daddy had cleared in front of our door, the next door—very unusual—and was clearing the backup in front of Mr. Willie's. Mr. Willie came out. They argued. Mr. Willie hit Daddy with a shovel. More than once someone described how Daddy's right eye was hanging out of the socket. Eventually he got a glass eye.

Several events around this incident took up a lot of my thought time: Daddy really was in the right—many of my memories about him definitely have him in the wrong. Even when I can honestly say I understand, I still conclude he was wrong. As far back as I could remember, Daddy had always said, "Don't let me be blind; I can put up with anything but bein' blind." He had always said that, and now, here he was blind in one eye. He never talked to me about it, but even now I think, "He really was right."

While I was in college, Daddy bought a piece of property. I know because he bought it in my name. He was sure that anything he bought in his name would be taken to finish the debt that the little green Pontiac started repaying.

About a year before I graduated, he had a house built. I had gone to college for one reason, to buy M'Dear a house. I will always believe he decided to act at that time because he knew I would make good my promise and build the house. But what had crossed his mind but never mine—honest—was that I would not let him live in the house. (He never knew how M'Dear always had something good to say to me about him. I would fuss; I would tell her she should leave him. I would cry. My interminable headaches would worsen. She would listen to my list of his "crimes" and then say, "But he wasn't always like that." My response was always, "But he's like that now, M'Dear!") I was simply glad that M'Dear had a house. She had always wanted to have the usher Christmas party at her house, but there was never any room. Now she could, and did.

What I heard and feel sure that Daddy had also heard was that I had bought the house. No one believed he had purchased it. One neighbor asked, "Didn't you buy that house?" I told her no, no, indeed. She said she knew me, and that I was just the type to buy the house and let everyone think Daddy had bought it.

My short visits did not show Daddy any different in the new house, his greatest achievement. If he ever thought about Mr. Beal, the little green car, or Mr. Willie, no one knew. He never mentioned them. The house, the car, five rooms of furniture, the yard—all belong to him. He would sit in the rocking chair or maybe the swing. He was satisfied. He read the paper; he always got the newspaper. He would watch the television. He always loved the news, baseball, and boxing. He listened to the radio, especially the baseball games and Jack Benny. He would visit Grandma and his sister. He would run errands for Grandma, always charging her $2.00 for the gas. Once or twice a year he would go to church.

One day in a very loud voice Daddy called, "Geor...... gia! Geor......... gia!" She came running, thinking, knowing something was terribly wrong. Ever so calmly, he was sitting in the rocking chair, slowly moving back and forth.

Out of breath, but seeing he looked fine, she asked, "What's wrong? What do you want?"

His answer: "Ain't 'm livin', Georgia? Ain't 'm livin'?"

1991

The Day She Changed the Radio

The car radio was blaring oldies but goodies. A number of the stations catering to the over-thirty crowd had gone out of business, so it was usually no radio or radio she did not really hear. The tape deck had long been broken. So it was great to hear this music she had matured by and with. She found herself smiling one of those Mona Lisa smiles. But she didn't think of the smile as enigmatic. She knew why she was smiling and did not mind divulging why to anyone who might have asked. But then no one would have ever thought to ask. This was a private, a very personal triumph.

At thirty-five she had not only the amenities of many in the American middle class—house, job, car—but also what she deemed important: health, family, and friends. She considered herself blessed physically, mentally, financially, and spiritually.

Joyce is one of those women who was independent long before independence became fashionable. She had to be. Too many depended on her, even when she was a kid. She had never had the luxury of expecting someone else to do what she needed to have done. But the subject of independence arises only when others mention it. For Joyce sees all of her actions as simply doing what she has to do, being responsible. Why ask someone to do for her when she can do for herself? There was nothing to explain. There was nothing special about the way she lived her life.

Getting married was no reason for her not to be independent. And husband never did anything to make her believe she could depend on him.

He refused to put dishes in the dishwasher because, he said, "You have a dishwasher." He never picked up a loaf of bread or carton of milk at the grocery: "I do not like to stop on my way home from work." Cooking and washing—putting the clothes in the washer and dryer—was woman's work. Cleaning the bathtub "wasn't really necessary." "Why do you want to make the bed? You get back in it every night." He always had a reason for whatever he didn't do. However, he always had the oil changed. He could be counted on to wash the car. He always hated a dirty car.

But another something he always did with no protestation was fix the car radio to go to a particular station. Whenever she wanted a station, he would punch it in. More than once she asked him to tell her how to do it, but he never did, and it never took long. It had never occurred to her to look in the manual. Perhaps he had always been there when she wanted to change stations.

But she wanted to keep this station. So she dug out the manual.

> To Set the Pushbuttons—When you are receiving a station, that you wish to commit to pushbutton memory, press the SET button. The letter P will show in the display window. Select the button you wish to lock on this station and press and release that button. If a button is not selected within 6 seconds after pressing the SET button, the station will continue to play but will not be locked into pushbutton memory.

She read it again. Let's see. She did it! Wow! It's so simple. How many years had it been since she first learned this could be done? Why hadn't she ever done it before?

The answer was simple. Whenever she had asked how to set a station, he had always done it. And she had asked many times. He had always done it. Here was something she could count on his doing. Why hadn't he told her? Maybe he considered it his secret. Was this power? Maybe he never thought about it. Maybe it was simply something he could do and he did. Maybe it never occurred to him that she really wanted to know how to do it. Why is this so important to her? And after so many years?

Years earlier she had been amazed when he explained his function as a husband. He had said clearly, "I go to work every day. I don't stay out late, and I don't throw away the money." Only after he said it did she realize how clear his definition really was. She hadn't known how well she had accepted it. And for a long time she did accept it. She admits to herself that she is still amazed. But at least she stopped accepting the definition long before she learned to program the radio stations.

Whatever.... The woman punches in her stations now, and she gets the greatest feeling! Maybe she'll punch in some she doesn't want simply to be able to punch them in—or out! Something so little to so many amazed her!

There's no telling what this woman will do!

1991

Letter to M'Dear

November 2008

Dear M'Dear,

Everyday for more than thirty-eight years I have thought about you. I sometimes speak silently to you; other times I talk as if you are here next to me rather than in the cemetery or heaven. There's so much I want to tell you, but then I think you know all about me and what's happening to me. But this news is a first. I have never felt the need to write you. But I want to make sure you know Barak Hussein Obama is the 44th president of the United States of America. Yes, you got that right! President, M'Dear. A black man is president. (Would you believe how often someone emphasizes the fact he's biracial? What happened to one drop of blood making a person black? He has 50% of undiluted black blood.) Anyway, you know me well. You know that I did not vote for him because he is black, despite what some may believe. But your favorite child and millions of other Americans believe this man ought to be president.

Have you heard him speak, M'Dear? He speaks so well. You know how I love words, how I unabashedly admit I love words, how

I believe any conflict can be solved if the parties talk about it honestly. And to those who say his speeches are "just words," "just eloquent," I say, "What do we have other than words?" Millions have been killed in the name of peace, and still there is little peace. I say every conflict which has ever ended with survivors on both sides came eventually to a point where words ended it. I say without qualification the pen is mightier than the sword. This man knows this truth and will practice it.

I believe him, M'Dear. I know he's a politician and the word "politician" is often said with derision, but this man is the politician of politicians. How did he get to this position? Can you believe he beat Hillary Clinton and all of the machinery and experience behind her? Do you remember how no one expected Bill Clinton to win the nomination the first time he got it? Scrappy Bill won and never thought he could not get this win for his wife. But Obama beat Mrs. Hillary Rodham Clinton. Obama beat John McCain with all of that McCain experience and a POW record yet to be completely revealed. To win, Obama had to play this game better than anyone else played. And he did. His middle name is Organization. The more I learn about how he captured this position, the more amazing the capture is. He is so different from everyone who was running, everyone who ever ran. He had to be. He has to be. He worked twice as hard as whites, maybe harder than any presidential candidate has ever worked. Everyday, all through the day, I marvel at this miracle.

I want everyone to know this man is president. Three months have passed, and I continue to think of persons I want to know: you first; Principal Morris H. Carroll; English teacher Mr. Thomas Ray Grant; math teacher Mr. Jack Wagner; Goodman, Cheney, and Schwerner; Emmett Till's mom; Emmett Till; Booker T. Washington; W. E. B. DuBois; Rosa Parks; Louis Armstrong; Viola Liuzzo; Ray Charles; Jackie Robinson; Frederick Douglass; Shirley Chisholm, Thurgood Marshall; Fannie Lou Hamer; James Brown and Curtis Mayfield. You know Dr. Martin Luther King, Jr. and Rev. Ralph Abernathy are givens as are the Kennedys. And M'Dear, tell Daddy—you remember how he told us "When the white folks get ready for you to go to the 'liberry,' they will let you go"—how he refused to get my two sisters released from detention when they were arrested for going to the white library. So much was white and colored. Oh, M'Dear, I never confessed to you about when I was eight I broke the law by drinking from the white water fountain, never told anyone until I was in college where I met many others who had done the same.

Back to the election. Two subjects pain me: the terrible predicament in which the country and world are and the number of persons who do not understand what the election means to so many of us. The wars—note the "s." The U. S. is fighting two wars, and neither foe endangered us. Nobody knows how many persons have died or been injured. The economy is reeling—the mortgage companies, the banks, unemployment, pension funds, and now the auto companies. Remember "As GM goes, so goes the country." This seems true, but for the first time in a negative mode. The weakened and failing infrastructure is countrywide. The number of children getting good educations through public schools decreases. Obama's tasks are Herculean. And at the same time, he has given more hope to more persons than many of us have ever had. Over the years many of us have worked hard. You know I worked with the Freedom Riders to register voters when I was a teen-ager; I have made a number of civic contributions, not the least of which is teaching at a community college more than thirty years. What I have done lately is a good example of Obama's influence. This is the first time I went to several caucuses, campaigned to be a delegate, donated to a presidential candidate, wore a button for a president, collected buttons (over 300, M'Dear), made calls, canvassed. I don't know how many hours I spent working on the campaign at home and at Obama headquarters. More people than ever in our history can say the same and/or make a longer list of what they have done. I went to the National Democratic Convention in Denver; I who had never wanted to go, just wanted Jessie Jackson supporters to be seated. So many people, black and white, red and brown cried when he was elected. I don't know if any president has ever had so many folks—in America and abroad—wishing him success. Babies know his face and name, M'Dear. This is why I wrote you.

When I think about all of the events I wanted you to celebrate here with us—the births of grandchildren and great-grandchildren, marriages, graduations, and so forth—the election of Obama is the most amazing, the most far-reaching. Remember all of those times you and teachers told all of us kids we could become president? Did you really know? How could you have known?

I never dreamed this dream. I still miss you and love you more than ever. You have my permission to share my letter with anyone in heaven.

Your namesake,

Georgia Lee

P. S. I read your letter to an all-white audience a few weeks ago. The eighty-year-old featured artist said he was reading his next poem because of my letter; his poem was a tribute to Obama. When he finished, he asked if I would tell you to share your letter with his mom.

11/24-25/08

2/11/09 Revised

Fishtailing

Fishtailed. That's exactly what the trailer home did. It swung to the left. And then it swung to the right. It did it again. It won't stop. I can certainly see why what the trailer is doing is called "fishtailing."

So this is the dream trip which ceased to be a dream for me a long time ago. Perhaps I exaggerate when I say the trip is a nightmare. But I don't think so. My God, when is the trailer going to stop? It keeps swishing from side to side. Surely this will soon stop. I am petrified. Sitting next to me, my husband is yelling, "Push the accelerator. Push the accelerator." We are dying. And he speaks to me in that same voice he has used all of our married life. If you heard him and did not see me, you would guess I was a naughty little child. You would never guess from his tone that I am a sixty-three-year OLD woman, only three years younger than he. I have never said, "Please don't talk to me like that. I am an adult. I have feelings. I have opinions. We don't have to agree, but I, too, can express myself." Why should I say it now? All of the years I didn't say it seem to be staring at me. It's true. Your life really does flash before your eyes. What happened? What happened to my life I mean. I should be asking why did the trailer begin to fishtail. But I have as little control over it as

I have had over my life. Asking why serves no purpose as the trailer keeps swaying back and forth.

When I was seventeen and he was twenty-one, I had such hopes. Ours would be the most wonderful life. We did not know each other very well. But our families had been friends for years. When he decided to go away to make his fortune, we hastily married. Since he was older and the male, he probably just as easily became accustomed to making decisions for us as I became accustomed to letting him make them. He told me what to wear; he told me what to cook. He told me when to cook. He decided when and where, how long I could or could not stay anywhere. It seems that I protested long ago, but I know I stopped the protesting almost as long ago. He has this air that says, "I know what I think, feel, or say is THE way to think or feel, speak. I know what ought to be said." She remembered the time she wanted to see a play and he said, "You saw that." She wanted to explain that she felt some plays deserved to be seen again and again, but she didn't. She remembered when she packed tennis rackets and balls in the car trunk only to arrive at their destination eight hours later and discover them not there. Since he was standing near her when she placed them in the trunk, she asked where were the balls and rackets. His explanation was simple: "You don't need to play tennis." On another occasion when she excitedly suggested that they go to a festival, he let her plan and plan. After she had gotten tickets and a couple to accompany them, he said, "It does not make sense to go that far to see a play." The night before the trip he said, "I won't go." For the first time in the three-year marriage she said, "I'll go with them" only to have him confidently chide, "You can't drive that far."

She replied, "Cam drives long distances all of the time. She can do it. I can help her." For some reason she was not backing down this time, a first. She expressed her feelings although she later felt certain he had not heard her. The next morning he refused to get ready. She walked out of the house just as Cam was driving up. Only after she got in the car did he slowly and sullenly walk down the stairs. He succeeded in making the trip hell. Knowing how she hated being cold, he kept the air conditioner on "high" throughout the trip.

Oh yes, and there was the time she was standing in the check-out line when she remembered she needed a lemon. He told her she did not need one. She said she would be back shortly; she needed only one lemon. But he snarled in that authoritarian voice, "You don't need a lemon." Speechless, she remained in the line.

The most belittling incident she remembered most was his teaching her to drive. She was twenty-three. Although she had taken driver education in high school she had not driven outside of the class; she, like the other fifteen students, had driven fifteen minutes twice a month. Yet he couldn't see why she couldn't drive. But he was willing to teach her. They had been driving around the neighborhood on two occasions. He would drive somewhere, get out, and tell her to drive. All he said was, "Drive." His next words—always a shout—would tell her what she was doing wrong. But during the third outing he calmly told her to pull over to the side of the street. She was waiting for the shouting. In the most imperturbable manner he said, "There are some things some people cannot do. You will never learn to drive. Get out." She did.

Weeks later through huge sobs she told her big sister about the incident. It was the big sister who taught her to drive. Sister had one rule: stay in your lane. At least two years passed before the husband would let his wife drive with him in the car. The trailer did its fishtailing one more time.

She remembered how she always laughed when she saw the title "One Life to Live." She knew for a fact that some people live more than one life—they take other people's lives, or, worse, other people give up their lives. For the first time she thought about the ones who simply GIVE away our lives. She was in that group she now knew.

She can't control the vehicle. Can't she at least think of something pleasant?

The lavish trailer had been "home" for about a month. The impetus for purchasing the trailer had been a visit to friends Les and Sal, owners of an extremely large motorhome. Listening to their stories of touring convinced them that they too wanted a motorhome. She had reluctantly agreed but thought this would be a great time to make their marriage better. The motorhome was what she wanted. Her vision included a long leisurely journey where they went off on every interesting exit. They had the money and the time. Daydreaming about this trip had occupied many of her hours. But she soon realized that his vision—and thus the actuality—was somewhat different from her own. Yes, she knows now she should have known. It was as if he were participating in a marathon! He wanted to see how fast he could get where so he could tell his buddies. He had a tight schedule, one he had neglected to discuss with her. All of her suggestions—all five of them—had been blasted before she could quite get them out.

What worsened the situation was his insistence that she drive. She never liked driving. His harsh criticism of her every movement made her avoid driving whenever she could. But, according to him, this lengthy trip had made not driving virtually an impossibility. He said nothing prevented her from driving. She had wanted to say, "You prevent me; you prevent me from doing all kinds of things." But, as usual, she hadn't. She thought about the forty years earlier when he was teaching her to drive. Now he was telling her she was always going too slow. Sometimes she was too far left or too far right. Very often she agreed with his assessments, but she was unable to make him see that his constant comments only made her uneasy and nervous. Being uneasy and nervous made her drive worse—at least according to his standards. Still, on this dream trip she had been driving a spell daily.

For some reason she seldom thought of the compliments she got about her driving. She was always surprised when anybody complimented her, but she was especially pleased when a man said she was a good driver. Her brother-in-law told her she backed the car into the carport "like a man." A male friend had said, "I went to sleep and slept well. I never sleep when other people drive." On another occasion, this man's wife assured me that he never slept while she drove. And there were other comments, none of which the speakers ever knew how much she appreciated. This morning he had started her driving earlier and made her continue longer, much longer than she wanted.

Now he was yelling, "Press the accelerator!" Though more frightened than she had been, she could not make her foot press the accelerator. She pressed the brake. She pressed the brake again. She pressed it a third time. Over went the big trailer being pulled by the big car. The trailer rammed the car into the guardrail. All she could think about was how little of her few accomplishments are actually her accomplishments. What she had done was go from Mom and Dad's house to husband's house. The house had probably been hers for a month before she realized that it was really his and not theirs. Maybe this was the price she paid for not taking the initiative at least on occasion. Now, because she had not said I don't feel comfortable pulling the trailer, she and he were piled against the guardrail. It was her fault. Though for some reason he was not speaking, she knew he was thinking if she had only followed his directions.... All she could think about was the minute amount of time she had lived her life her way. Feeling as if she was still swaying from side to side—very much like the trailer had done earlier—she realized that perhaps it was not too late to try to live her life. She just hoped she would have the chance.

1992

Impressions: The First Day of School

Finally! Finally he was going to school. It seemed he had spent all of his five years waiting to go to school. School must be a wonderful place. For years—or at least all of his life—his mom had been going. His brother had been going for as long as he could remember. Indeed, that sister who loved him so much had been going too. One could see why he would hate this place school because three persons who loved him deserted him five days a week to go to that place. But somewhere at some time, he had come to believe that school must be good. Everyone he loved was going. And he had to admit that everyone always returned to him! Every afternoon, each of them returned. And for one long period not one of them left the house! This happened ever so often. He didn't know why, but he was glad for it. Yes, this school thing was going to be good.

Now he had not always felt this way about school. In those days all he knew was that it was a place his mom went every day. On many occasions she had attempted to explain what school was, but he had not really understood. All he knew was that his mom left. He never wanted her to leave, but some days he did not want her to leave more than on other days.

He clearly remembered his worst day. His mom was leaving—to go to school, of course. She took him to the place where she always took him. There were always other people his size there; that was good. Somebody brought them too. He guessed it was their moms. These people, like him, never wanted those ladies to leave either. But most of the little people—like him—said "Bye" or waved. Quite a few of the little people cried or sniffled. But he did not cry. Oh, he wanted to. But there was something within him that prevented tears from coming.

On this day, however, when his mom leaned to kiss him on the cheek—she ALWAYS did that—his little hand slapped her as hard as his little hand could hit! He did hope it would hurt. He hadn't really planned to do this. But everyday his eyes seemed to demand that he cry, and everyday he had refused. He certainly was not going to let his mom know that water was so close to coming from his eyes. No, daily he had dutifully stood for the kiss. But not today. And as much as those tears tried to come, he held them back.

Of course, he would never know that his mom too managed to keep her tears back—until she returned to the car. She cried everyday as she drove the ten miles to her job at the school. By the time she walked in the building she was the composed kindergarten teacher that all of the children loved. But that's another story.

The day after he slapped his mom he took her leaving differently. He still hated her leaving. He still wanted her to stay with him. He really did not know what had changed, only that he dutifully got his kiss and resigned himself. He knew she would return. On those rare days when she did not come to pick him up, his dad would come. For some reason he seemed to know that he had to be satisfied that someone would get him. Eventually all five of them would be together again.

That was a long time ago; it's funny that he would remember it today. Yet he had. That was a sad day, but today was a happy day!

He was so proud to be leaving home not to go to that place—which really wasn't bad but was never home—but rather to go to school. He would not have to get out of the car while his sister and brother waited for his mom to leave him. And everything he had on was new: shirt, jeans, socks, shoes! Why, he also had on new underwear! It seemed he had more new clothes than he had ever had at one time. They were all in his closet just waiting for him. His dad had told him what a big boy he was. His sister had told him he would have fun. More important, she had told him she would find him at recess. He did not know what "recess" was, but knowing his sister would find him was sufficient. His brother chimed he would see him at the same time. Being with them was wonderful. He knew he was special. He was so happy. Knowing he was going to see them at that place made him happier.

How could he have hated this place so much? His mom had told him what happened there. She always smiled when she talked about this place. She told him about other people there, many just like him she said. He had had to admit that maybe he shouldn't have disliked it so much. What was probably true, he concluded eventually, was that what was bad was his mom's leaving. Perhaps school was ok.

He had passed by the place before, but he had never been in. This is a big place he thought as he walked through the doors. And he felt as important as the building seemed big. That his mom had come into the building and taken him to his class and left him all by himself increased his bigness. Now he was on his own! Was this the first time he had ever been anywhere—except the place he waited—with no family member there in the room with him? He thought it was. Why he is bigger than even he thought he was! He was so proud. This is a nice room. It is so bright and pretty. There are pictures all over the room. Some look like the ones he had helped his mom prepare at home. He knew what the pictures were. He knew some of the words on the wall too. Oh—there are the ABC's—bigger than he had ever seen them! He had learned them ages ago. He could write all of them; he could write most of them without following a guide. Oh, he was going to like this place. He thought: "Oh, my goodness. There are the numbers too!" He could write all of them all by himself. He could count to a hundred. There were boys and girls—all of them seemed to have on new outfits. Some looked a little sad, and one or two seemed to want to cry but refused. He understood that look. Today he would not look like that. He was sorry for those little people, but he was having a good time.

Oh, he must pay attention now. The pretty lady at the front of the room—the teacher his mom had called her—was about to read to them. He could not see the front of the book, but he did not care which book it was. All of his family read to him. Sometimes he chose the book; other times they chose. Most of the time it did not really matter. He loved everything about reading.

The teacher began. He liked her voice. She sounded a little like his mom. Not as good, of course, but still very good. The lady was ok. She looked at him, and sometimes she looked at the other kids too. He could tell she was enjoying reading the story.

He didn't believe it! This was a story he had heard. "Oh, my goodness," he thought. "I am going to love this place. Not only is she reading a story; she is reading a story I know, a story I have at home!" Nobody had told him she was going to read. And now she is reading a story he knows! All of his family members had read that story. His sister had probably read it more times than anyone. The smile on his little face got bigger and bigger. Maybe he should listen more carefully, just to be sure.

But just then the lady—the teacher his mom had told him—read: Cats here, cats there,

Cats and kittens everywhere

Hundreds of cats

Thousands of cats

Millions and billions and trillions of cats.

(*Millions of Cats*, Wanda Gag)

Yes, he was right! It was a story he knew so well. He knew exactly what was going to happen. Yes, he was going to like this place. Just then, he laughed out loud. He hadn't been able to laugh quietly. He loved that story. Maybe his mom had told the teacher which story to read.

But the teacher had stopped reading. "Ronald," she said.

My, oh, my, she knows my name! How wonderful, he thought.

"Yes," he said in the most grown-up voice he could muster.

"Ronald, this is not the time to laugh. We are reading now. You must get up. Go sit in the chair in the corner. I will tell you when you may rejoin the group."

He doesn't remember how he got to the corner. He had never had to sit in a corner before. He knew it wasn't good to sit in the corner. All of the bigness he had felt earlier had somehow disappeared. He felt so little now, littler than he really was. He had never felt so little. His mom and sister and brother and dad would not be pleased. He had no idea what he had done. Yet he knew he had done wrong. He wanted to be in his seat. He tried so hard to remember everything he had done. He kept coming up with the same thing: he had laughed out loud. No one had told him not to laugh. He always laughed when his mom or sister or brother or dad read a book. Why, they laughed too. Oh, if Teacher had told him not to laugh, he knows he would not have laughed. He could have done it. He always did what his mom said; he always did what the lady at the place where he had stayed everyday for what seemed all of his life said. She was always telling his mom what a wonderful child he was. His mom had told him to do what the teacher says. He had done everything. If someone could explain.... He wouldn't do it again. He sat there as the teacher continued reading. For everyone else nothing seemed to have changed.

Though he tried and he tried, he could not determine what he had done wrong.

1992

Jr.

I remember the day my brother Jr. left home. It was a Sunday. M' Dear and the five of us sisters and brothers were at church. Somebody came in to get her, said her son was outside.

I didn't leave with M'Dear, but as soon as I could, I slipped outside. I remember seeing blood on Jr. What made me stop I don't know. I simply stopped, startled. He had on a white, short-sleeved t-shirt. His pants—which had never seemed to fit his tiny body—were very dirty. He had on that always present blue baseball cap. It could have had Brooklyn Dodgers on it. He looked smaller than he had ever looked, and though he was my big brother and eleven years older, he had always seemed small physically. Now he seemed exceedingly small. But he and M'Dear were talking in a way that let this nine-year old know something was wrong. He was telling M'Dear that he had to leave. He needed some money.

Before I could butt in, one of the ushers, Mrs. Alma of all people—oh, how I would love to hear her story; she forever rubbed us kids the wrong way—told my sister and me to go back inside. All of this must have taken two minutes. I wanted so much to run to my brother, but Mrs. Alma had told us to go back inside. And because we grew up in a time when youngsters obeyed any adult, and usually didn't mind, we went inside.

Later my mom said that Jr. had left. At my insistence, she confessed that he was leaving town. I knew she had not wanted to tell me. But both she and I knew that she had to tell me. At least she assured me that he would be all right.

I missed him more than I could ever have imagined. All of my life he had lived with M'Dear's mom, Mama, so I did not spend a lot of time with him, but when I was first grade and he was eleventh, he had walked the mile or so from our grandmother's to our house every morning and walked me to school. It was just the two of us. I always felt so big when I was with him. We never held hands. We just talked. We always had the best conversations. I can't remember what most conversations were about. He never walked too fast, the way my aunt who was his age walked me every afternoon. I don't recall ever talking about a problem with him. Maybe I didn't have any. I do remember wishing he lived with us and being happy to have him all to myself. What I remember most is wishing we could walk forever. Being with him gave me such a good feeling. At school, he would find me at noon and give me some of whatever he had bought at the little store across the street, usually a sour pickle. It seems he always had an excuse to avoid sharing with everyone but me. I remember when he taught me how to fly a kite. I used to love to do that, but I never did it with anyone but Jr. Surely other kids must have been around, but I don't remember them. Another of his special treats always came at Easter. Although everyone at my house dyed Easter eggs in the morning, we knew not to discard the dye. My mom never considered pouring it out. You see, Jr. would show up with a dozen eggs—sometimes as late as 8:00 p.m. or 9:00 p.m. We gleefully dyed them as if they were the first eggs we had ever dyed. He would also have a chocolate bunny—a solid chocolate bunny. I never eat solid chocolate without thinking about him. And I don't eat it too often. There was always a Christmas present too. I still have the doll he bought me the last Christmas before he left.

I did not see him again for years, but he would call several times a year. When he came home, I was away. When I came home, he was away. But I ALWAYS sent him a birthday card and a Christmas card. I do not recall ever having a card or letter returned. After several years I started writing on the cards, "This is the last time I am going to write if you do not answer me." He never answered, and I never stopped sending the cards, sometimes with a note, other times with only my "I'll never write again" note.

Then M`Dear died in 1970, and he came to the funeral. That's the one time in our lives that all eight of her children were together. M'Dear never saw all of us in one setting. As much as I wanted to see Jr., M'Dear's death took precedence. So he and I never got a chance to talk for very long. Everybody's life changed, and in various ways each of us had our coping to do. It seems all of us must have thought the best way to do it was not to talk about our tremendous loss. There's no doubt that her death left an indelible mark on each of us.

But from that time on, Jr. and I contacted each other more often. I was in Seattle; he was in Newark, New Jersey, where I had learned he had lived since he left. He drove gasoline trucks for gas companies. He would call—always at night, usually at two or three in the morning. He would always say, "You sound sleepy." I would always say, "I was asleep." And then he would remember the time difference and apologize profusely. But a month or so later, we would begin another conversation the same way. It took years for me to realize that he was most likely—notice "most likely"—intoxicated when he called me.

By this time I could support myself. Actually I was rich! So, accompanied by a sister five years younger, I went to visit our brother. My sister had been to Newark; I had not. She kept telling me not to get my hopes up. She had seen the place where he lived, and it was not a place I would be comfortable, she said. She never used the word "ghetto." But I soon learned that was what she was referring to. I was an adult before I recalled hearing people say, "There are no ghettoes in the South. You have to go North to see a ghetto." As the cab drove by the rows of buildings with crooked windows, no windowpanes, and sagging doors, I knew exactly what had been meant. Men of all ages were standing on or sitting at the corner. Many were simply talking. Others were playing checkers or dominoes.

Nothing would have ever made me believe that my brother was living in such a place, but he was. And our sister and I had found it. Perhaps it is good she had been there several years earlier—actually when she lived in New York, I had suggested that she visit him, and she had.

As we entered the apartment, we saw sitting on the couch a woman who looked older than our mom would've been. Something told me she was the "Mary" I had talked to so many times. She was a little woman, short. She seemed round from head to foot. She had beautiful, smooth black skin. It would be years before I learned she was exactly twenty years older than my brother, older than our mother. The two of them had been together at least twenty years.

He was as small as ever. But he still had the face of the high school Jr. who walked me to school. He was so happy to see both of us, but I got the bigger hug. Really.

I could smell alcohol although I tried not to smell it. Again, although there had been many calls that convinced me that he had been drinking, I never thought about his being an alcoholic. Our sister and I sat down, and after a few minutes of discomfort—probably because the place was so dirty—we asked and answered questions. It was here that I learned that ten-year-old Bridey—a child whom I considered a niece—was not really his daughter. She belonged to a woman who at one time had lived next door. The woman was an alcoholic, and her parenting skills clearly showed she was not a recovering alcoholic! Jr. and Mary were forever fussing at the mother because they did not believe she was giving the baby proper care. One or the other of them would simply hear the baby crying, get up, and go next door either to fuss at the mother about not taking care of the baby or take care of the baby. This evidently went on the first few months of the baby's life. Then one day the two of them went over prepared to give another lecture. The mom interrupted. She put the baby in Mary's arms and told them to take the baby and get out.

That is exactly what they did. The child had been with them ever since, about ten years.

Neither my sister nor I was truly comfortable in that room. What served as a carpet was terribly dirty; no one should have had to walk on it. Grease seemed to pour out of it. Neither Jr. nor Mary seemed to notice. We continued to talk about the family and all of the time we had been apart. What I wanted to know most was why hadn't he written me. He got up, went to a chest of drawers, opened one, and then removed a plastic bag full of cards. He took out a few of the cards as he sat next to me. Amazed, I looked at the many cards I had sent over the many years. I noted how the fourth grade handwriting got steadier and steadier. I also noted how often I had put exactly the same note on the cards. And he had kept each and everyone! Not one piece of mail had come from anyone else. All were from me! I never asked if anyone else had written. I could not believe that he had saved all of my correspondence. Some cards were at least twenty-three years old.

Somehow much of his environment no longer had an effect on me. I who had never doubted that my brother loved me discovered that the love was far greater than anything I could ever have imagined. I convinced myself that the letters/cards had sustained him in the same way the sending of them had sustained me. The first-grade closeness was alive and well.

My sister reminded me that we had to get back. Gladly and sadly, I left him. Seeing him that day is still one of the highlights of my life.

The calls came more frequent—always late at night or early in the morning and often in a slur. Never once did I wish he had not called. But I always wished he hadn't felt the need to drink or at least to drink so much. Now I talked to Mary and Bridey more often. Having faces to go along with the voices made the conversation easier.

The next big event to connect us was Daddy's death. For a number of varied reasons four of the eight of us chose to go to the funeral in Louisiana and four of us did not attend the services. No one seemed to be surprised that I stayed in Seattle but gave the others money to go. The big surprise for me was Jr.'s attendance. When I saw him two years later, I was still wondering why he had gone to Daddy's funeral. Sometimes I think my curse is asking why. Though this may seem odd, Daddy had an odd relationship with each of us—odd as in not good. And all of us knew that at an early age. As an adult I still try to make sense of this. I know enough about Daddy to understand that he did the best he knew how, but I still consider it much too little. But, based on what I knew, I had his relationship with Jr. pegged perfectly: as M'Dear's son from an earlier marriage, Jr. was not welcomed by Daddy. Daddy said very little about Jr., but as a youngster I always knew he treated Jr. differently from the way he treated the rest of us. This is not to say that the rest of us were treated with great kindness. But Jr.'s going to the funeral had knocked me off balance. I could not ask him why he went over the phone, but the next time I saw him, I could not resist.

His answer came forth immediately and clearly: "One day Missy, [our older sister] and I were eating. I was about ten; she was eight. There was one biscuit left on the table. I wanted it. But as Missy often did, once I said I wanted something, she yelled she wanted it too. Both of us wanted it. M'Dear wanted to split the biscuit, but Missy wanted the whole thing. Daddy intruded. He said Missy should get what she wanted. He gave Missy the whole biscuit." Jr. said that on that day—he was ten years old—he decided that he would see dirt thrown in Daddy's face. And he did.

It was here that I concluded my poor brother's life had been much worse than it looked. All these years—thirty-six at least—he had walked around hating Daddy. If he ever blamed M'Dear for marrying Daddy or his alcoholic father for not staying with them, he never told me about it. He never mentioned his daddy. He knew our grandmother loved him. I think he knew M'Dear loved him. But there must have been some sense of rejection; everybody was with M'Dear but him. Once he had been her only companion. I know he knew I loved him. Even now I don't know why he and I never talked about seeing each other more often. He just called ever so often. I tried calling, but his phone was usually disconnected. I soon settled for letting him call me. Sometimes one of our sisters would tell me that Jr. had called her. But, she always said, "He said I called Joy, and she wasn't home, so I called you." Another sister was fond of telling me that he said, "I called Joy, and she wasn't there. I called Valerra, and she wasn't there, so I called you." The sisters always made it clear to me that he had an order of calling from which he never veered. What seems like rivalry to some never seemed to be the case with us. It was understood that he wanted to talk to me first. Ours was a relationship that I feel certain all of them knew was between the two of us and different from their relationships. The three-year difference between him and Missy had probably made it impossible for them to have the kind of relationship he and I had. And the other three sisters were fourteen, fifteen, and twenty-four years younger than he. They could not possibly know him as I had known him. That he always tried to get me first and called them only after failing to get me became a joke. I was always sorry to miss him but very glad that he had talked to someone. More than once I told him not to tell them he had called me first, but he never seemed to remember.

About two years after that first visit, his doctor called me. A doctor calling someone was not something I had heard of. But his doctor in New Jersey called me in Seattle. She explained that Jr. had esophageal cancer. She said he had been in the hospital about two months and that I should come to see him. I don't remember too much about preparing to go—only that if I waited a week I could get a lower priced ticket. I checked with the doctor who assured me that I could wait a week. That flight still ranks as the longest one I have ever taken. The doctor, now that I thought about it, had not told me very much. But there was something that had made me know that I had to go.

Finally I arrived in Newark and went straight to the hospital. Before I could see the doctor whom I had asked for by name, a nurse said, "You must be Allen's sister." It took a moment to realize that she was talking about my brother. It seems everyone here called him by his last name, a name no one used at home. The nurse said she had been looking forward to seeing me because she had heard so much about me. My look must have said please get me the doctor.

My anxiety obviously was out in full force now. However, before the doctor came, I was introduced to several other people who had heard about "Allen's sister."

After what seemed like eternity, I talked with the doctor who explained what was wrong. She said the cancer was steadily growing. I wanted to know why they couldn't remove it. She explained that removing it was impossible, that had it been discovered earlier, it more than likely could have been removed. But now, it had attached itself to vital organs, his heart and lungs. There was no way surgeons could cut anything. For the same reason they could not do very much treatment with chemotherapy or radiation.

Why hadn't he noticed it? "Well," she replied, "he hadn't felt it. He came to the hospital when he began having problems swallowing." Esophageal cancer is generally the result of smoking cigarettes and drinking alcohol. My brother did both—heavily. He smoked Camels. And, she added, "A third reason is pollution. Newark, New Jersey, has the highest rate of esophageal cancer in the United States." In the kindest, most gentle voice, she said the cancer was "like a bulldozer, moving slowly but steadily." It was constricting his lungs, his throat. Eventually he would not be able to breathe. Everything was against him, she explained. I don't know if she had finished; I just know that I had to see him.

With the driest eyes and calmest face, I slowly walked to his room. What I saw I later described as looking exactly like Yoda of Star Wars fame. I could probably have counted the strands of hair on his head, hair not its natural black but rather an ugly combination of red and brown. His always small body was smaller still. His hands were so bony; they looked like the hands of a very old, skinny, sickly woman I had known. I saw all of this before he could say anything to me. But his smile showed me that he was in extremely good spirits. He called the nurse to tell her he had told her I would come. He had been hospitalized long enough for many of the patients and staff to know him. Actually, it seemed everyone knew him. What amazed me was how everyone "knew" me too. I never knew how long he had been hospitalized. But he had been strong enough to walk around pushing his Porta-Cast of medicine steadily dripping into his veins, and evidently everybody who spent anytime talking to him had to hear about his sister.

Three days after I arrived, our sister who had accompanied me to his home two years earlier arrived from Louisiana. At the airport, she abruptly stopped me, "I am here for you," she said as emphatically as she could. Her stern face showed she meant business; it was as if she did not want to be there, but I was there, so she was. As much as I hated that she felt as she did, I knew her love for me had brought her to my side. I also knew she had been about five when he left.

At least twice someone told her—and many more times someone told me—that they thought I was his only living relative. He had never mentioned anyone else. Surprised, I quickly explained that there were three more sisters and two more brothers. Somehow it did not matter.

I spent all day everyday with my brother. He told me he had been through a lot and he always beat it. He was going to beat this too. I think he really believed it. I wanted to believe it so much, but I never did. He was going to come to Seattle and see us, he said. He knew he should have come earlier, but he was really coming. His voice was fine. He had long since stopped eating solids. He could drink very little. He had difficulty swallowing. By the time I left, he would not be able to swallow his saliva.

After almost two weeks I had to leave. I got a big hug, but it wasn't nearly as good as it should have been; I was too afraid I would hurt him. I can feel it now when I decide to. With the strongest voice, he said he would see me. I could always get him at the hospital, so I called often and told him to call me any time he wanted. We talked more regularly than ever—that is since those days when I was in the first grade and he was in the eleventh. But the doctor was right; the bulldozer of a cancer was steadily moving.

1992

Nobody Asked Her

Joy was one of the people who had not always understood why a person would not want to go to a high school reunion. She had learned only after listening to tales told by a few friends—how some ancient childhood grudges were not buried, how insecurities in kids had often simply grown with the kids rather than disappeared, how what some would have called imagined fears weren't, after all, imagined. She could understand, but she could not understand why her class had not had a reunion. She had been a bit disappointed when the fifth year passed and no one had said anything about having one, but she never mentioned it. She quickly reasoned that it wasn't so terrible. And although she had hoped there would be a tenth year reunion, she hadn't been too surprised when there wasn't. She told a few classmates how she felt. But even she knew that her enthusiasm and desire were not enough to organize a reunion long distance from Seattle. Joy had actually been to Monroe and tried to put one together herself but had been unable to get any of her Monroe friends to take the reins. However, she had managed to get about fifteen classmates to have dinner together and then meet at a friend's house where they talked about a reunion. This was later referred to as a "mini-reunion" by some although Joy never labeled it such. Fifteen of the 150 members of the Class of '63 was not a reunion!

When she had received word of an upcoming reunion, she immediately called Dean, the organizer, to see what she could do. He needed addresses. Joy, acknowledged information keeper of the class, was the one who supposedly had the best memory and, therefore, knew where many members could be found. Remembering that one classmate had told her she even knew where people were buried, she happily sent every address she had and waited patiently for more news.

It was only after she wrote her brother and told him about the reunion that she realized it would be their eighteenth reunion. He complained that no one has an eighteenth reunion! "Why won't you wait until the twentieth?" he queried.

Her reply was, "Have it when we can. Maybe we can have another in two years." She had said she was twenty-three so long that she had forgotten they were all in their thirties. Most amazingly, she had not realized just how many classmates she had not seen since graduation. Theirs had been the largest class ever, but it was during the days when classes increased yearly. Because she knew so many parents and siblings and received the hometown newspaper, she had ceased thinking of them as a class, but often called on birthdays and received the latest happenings.

OK, so maybe nobody had had eighteenth year reunions, but then it was just like the Class of '63. It had always been different. And as far as Joy could tell, this had worked to no one's detriment. Class members are in any professions she could think of. They live all over the world. Seven of them live in Seattle.

She was not going to think about which reunion, only that she was glad she would be seeing so many of the people who had been so important in her life. She would rather go to school than stay at home. This list of important people included classmates and teachers. At the top of the list was Mr. Henry Carroll, the principal. Although he had been dead over two years—died when she was out of the country—she still could not think about him without being sad.

She had never told him what a tremendous impact he and Carroll High had and still have on her life. Many who know her know this, but he didn't. But thank goodness many of the teachers would be there; most still live there. More and more she thought about what fun the trip would be. But then visiting Monroe was always fun. If her mom were still alive, Monroe would probably be near perfect! Wisely, she put such thoughts out of her head.

What preoccupied her was the simple fact that the result of all the work by the handful of classmates was about to become a reality. She was in Monroe for the real thing; everything was set. Lovers of Carroll High School—to her anyone who ever attended was a lover—were coming from all over the country and some from other countries.

Seeing everybody would be great fun. A wonderful program had been planned. There was a picnic, a banquet, church, a social, and a disco. She looked forward to everything! The only event she really thought about was the disco. She knew she was going, but it did occur to her that the greatest part of her fun at the disco would probably be talking to everyone. After all these years she could still count the few times she had danced in high school. She did not let herself forget that the disco would not be the only event.

She and a number of other out-of-towners had actually arrived in town several days early. Kenneth, Sandra Kay, Dorothy Faye, Woodard, Joy. They had all known each other since first or second grade. But then Monroe is one of those places where it was common for kids to have the same classmates throughout their school years and sometimes go to college together. Although three of them lived elsewhere—Atlanta, Oakland, and Seattle—all admitted that it had never occurred to them not to come to the reunion.

And now she and these friends were sitting in Willie T.'s , a place she had never frequented when in high school because it was for adults. Everybody was excited. Everybody looked good—honest. Joy could see no big differences. Everybody was happy. Of the five, she talked to Sandra, a junior high teacher, most often. And since Sandra had been seriously ill a few years earlier, Joy had called her more often. They also corresponded. Faye, the operator of a nursing home, gets a birthday call every year. She too writes, but not as often. Faye and Sandra frequently call Joy on what they think is Joy's birthday, and she never feels compelled to tell them that she was not born on Christmas Day. Kenneth gets a call too, but because he is a minister, he is often not home. His wife and Joy have become good friends. Kenneth was probably her closest male friend; they were in first through twelfth grades together. As members of Homeroom Twelve-One, they had played a pivotal role in almost everything on campus. It was Kenneth's idea that she be class business manager—a position classes had never had—rather than president because Miss Carroll would need an escort. It never bothered her. She knew Kenneth wanted to be president. Woodard, a cabinetmaker, sometimes gets a call on his birthday. For a long time she had not known where he was. Then she got in touch with his mom. So sometimes she called his mom on his birthday. What she remembered most about him is how he loved to draw. During sixth grade he would draw, and Joy would color his drawings. She always thought they made a good team. Curtis Mayfield must have had this kind of feeling when he penned "My life's a natural high."

As an adult living in a big city she now knew how rare it is to have so many good friends. She relished listening to their tales. Eventually the conversation got to the scheduled events. Joy commented, "The disco should be fun."

Surprised, Faye answered with, "Joy, did you ever learn to dance?"

Never missing a beat, Joy replied, "I could dance. No one ever asked me." Everybody laughed. Joy smiled. She had stated the plain truth.

Then the discussion was on the music, all of those sixties songs that most of the group knew from memory. Somebody was always asking about someone or remembering some significant event—a few sad, most happy. They had always been told that high school was the best time of their lives. They might not have agreed when they heard the statement, but at least this five believed those days to be some of the best.

About midnight, the group decided to go to their various homes because the next day would be a busy day.

Finally the night of the disco, Faye's birthday, arrived. Joy—and probably most of the alumni—had never been to the Ramada Inn. She couldn't even remember if the Ramada Inn had been there when they were in school. Then Blacks went in such places only because they were on the service staff. Although she had made a conscious effort not to think about the way it was, she occasionally found herself thinking about the marks segregation had left on so many. There were so many differences in Monroe, and to a visitor the differences looked good. Most of the thoughts at the time were pleasant. Dancing wasn't on her mind: seeing all of those people was uppermost. Classmates who had called or come by her aunt's alerted her that the gathering would be good. Rumor had it that the largest percentage of graduates ever would be attending. Sadly most of the people not coming were people who lived in Monroe. By now she had talked to a number of people whom she really wanted to see.

When she and Sandra drove up and saw the big lighted sign saying "Welcome, Carroll High Class of '63" her thoughts were of pleasantries only. She had tried very hard to be there at eight, but for several reasons—among them taking a picture of the billboard—the best she could do was 8:15 p.m.

They could hear the Temptations before they entered the Holidome. Less than ten steps in the door, John Bowman, one of the football stars, asked Joy to dance. Startled, she said, "Let me put my purse down."

Sandra quickly butt in with, "I'll take it." Joy and John joined two or three other couples on the dance floor. Trying to dance and recognizing the long unseen faces was not easy, but she worked at it. The music ended, and as she had somewhere become accustomed to doing, she thanked him profusely. She was about to ask him where he was living and what he was doing when Harold Gray stepped up and asked for a dance. Harold was someone she had not thought about in all those years of separation. But she knew him immediately. After school during their senior and junior years, he had done custodial work, and she had posted insurance premiums for Miller Funeral Home. The dancing was fun, and the singing along made it better. As much as she was enjoying the dancing, she wanted to get to a table where she could greet classmates. Just as one record ended and she turned to find Sandra, football player Monroe Sims tapped her on the shoulder and asked for a dance. Monroe had been very popular. He had always spoken to her, but she was sure they had never had a conversation. Now he was asking her—Joy—for a dance. And all of those other girls—women—were there!

Some of the ones who had always—it seems—been glamorous were there. Joy had had many male friends throughout her school years. They talked to her; they called her. But the subject was always about proofreading a paper or, worse, assisting writing a paper or helping with a report, or giving an idea for a report, or doing a physics problem or a math problem. As an adult she came to think that the boys had seen her as a sexless creature. She still remembered how they gladly carried girls' books home but in four years of walking to school everyday only two boys—in their senior year—carried her books home. One was a transfer student, so she reasoned he must not have known that boys never carried her books home! But here was this boy that girls had fought over, here was this boy asking for a dance! She obliged. It was about then that she noticed another girl—Mary—whom she had never seen at a high school party; she was on the dance floor, very pregnant, and dancing the night away.

But back to herself, three dances—three consecutive dances—she had never had a chance to sit down! This was surely some error. She tried to tell herself to enjoy, don't think about how or why, just enjoy. Her mom had always told her if she wanted a boyfriend she could get one. She had never been bold enough to say, "But I do, but I do!" Nor had she been bold enough to try to explain further.

Then the record ended as another began, and Clarence Grayson, handsome, smooth-talking Clarence Grayson—another football player—was asking her to dance! She decided she would merely dance. She would devote no time to whys and hows. About the same time she noticed that Mary too was still dancing .

Now she knew what was happening. Kenneth, who had always been the organizer, after all these years was still organizing. He had always been able to get his classmates to do just about anything. He had heard Joy's very honest, open remark about never having been asked to dance, and he was doing something about it. She saw him with a little pad in his hand. He was making what appeared to be a check and directing another male classmate toward someone else. Joy made all of these observations as she listened intently to Marvin Gaye.

At the end of the tune, she started toward Kenneth only to be stopped by Sherman Butler. By anyone's standards, Sherman, she thought, was a hunk, but he asked her to dance! She had to oblige. One night at a dance in Seattle she had told a man how debilitating it was for a woman to get dressed, go out, and then sit all night waiting for a man to ask her to dance only to go home never having been asked. The man responded with something she had never thought about: he said it takes lots of nerve for a man to ask a woman to dance. Often he is with his friends, and he has to walk what seems like a mile to ask a woman to dance. Sometimes there are several women sitting together. Not only does the first choice turn him down, but so do the others. Then he has to walk all the way back to the group of men friends who do not let him forget that all of those women turned him down! This thought prevented her from saying no to any would-be dancer—the first time.

But since Sherman is the uncle of a classmate who had not come to the reunion, they discussed her whereabouts. Next was Euthell. He had been one-half of those campus-famous duos. Both had married others. With Gladys and the Pips going, Joy danced with Lorenzo. Then there was Ernest—a homeroom buddy. He was known to be one of the cutest guys on campus. And now approaching her was the assistant drum major—Johnny Jones. He danced so well. He would never have asked her to dance, but there he was, asking her to dance. Joe Fletcher, another football player. My goodness!

Val Jean—the drum major. He was tall and slender. And everyone knew he could dance. And with all of the majorettes and cheerleaders in the room—this man wanted to dance with Joy! And that's the way it went. Billy, a college buddy. George, Jerry—a guy whom Joy had always adored, Willie, another of those she met in first grade, homeroom mate John whose wife told Joy she was the one person she wanted to meet at the reunion—her husband had always said Joy was the kindest person he had ever known. Jake, a jokester who still occasionally calls with a joke, and then there was Kenneth.

She finally got a chance to talk to him. All he said was that they wanted Joy to dance. He did add that they thought she would have been tired after a few dances.

Last—but far from least—was Woodard. He said, "I always knew I should have married you" as they danced to Stevie Wonder's "I Was Made to Love Her."

One of the most wonderful nights of her life was over. She had danced every dance, the only person who had. Now awards were about to be presented. An award definitely not scheduled was made. Something they did not have to do but something which will forever be special to Joy was the presentation of a quickly made "dance book." On it salutatorian and lawyer Frances had gotten all of the men to sign their names. Kenneth—Joy would know that handwriting anywhere—had written beneath "Class of '63" something she will always cherish: "We didn't know!!!"

The next day at the Class Day activities—when there wasn't supposed to be any dancing—a classmate who had missed the previous night because he practices dentistry in the Philippines walked up to Joy. With the same slight hint of a stutter she remembered from high school, he said, "I, I, I, hear everybody here danced with you last night. I don't want to be left out. I, I want to sign that card, so let, let, let's dance!"

1981

No Day to Swim

Proud of the fact that she was at the recreational center on a Saturday morning doing her ten miles on the stationary bicycle, Jennie decided that rather than swimming laps she would join the aquarobics class. The company was fine, and the exercises were probably better than the swimming only. If she pedaled the stationary bike a little faster, she could make the class on time. It took working hard and much faster pedaling than she wanted, but the exercise would be worth it. She joined the group!

This was just one more reason for her to feel soooooo good! She was certainly on a roll. She couldn't remember the last time she had a bad day or even something unpleasant happen to her or those whom she knew and cared about. As sad as she was because everyone everywhere wasn't so fortunate, she thanked God again and jumped off the bike. Once more she chided herself about thinking something had to go wrong soon. There really isn't a law which says something has to go wrong; it just seemed that so much of her life had seemed to be that way, so she sometimes found herself thinking something had to go wrong any minute. But today was different; she was basking in the good feeling.

Now all she had to do was run in to the locker room, pull off the jumpsuit, get in the shower, and hop in the pool. She made it! Surely there was a reason for this exercise regiment, but the reasons escaped her at this time.

Then the music—which she often listened to as she was doing laps on the deep end rather than exercising in the shallow end—came on. What was that song? Even as she asked the question she knew the answer. You know how we sometimes ask questions to which we know the answers but we wish the answers were different? Of all the songs, why was that Atlas of a lifeguard instructor playing this one?

Of course, she knew what it was. It was "Since I Lost My Baby." She could have named it and all of the other Temptation songs in one note! But today! How could he play it today? Of all days!

This is her first time to hear a Temptations song since Eddie Kendricks died. Ever since she had been interested in music she had been interested in the Temptations. She knew they are older than she but not old enough to die—she recognized the absurdity of anyone being too young to die as the absurdity it was. She certainly knew better. For a long time she had known age and death are not necessarily directly proportional. Silly her. When she heard Kendricks was fifty-three, she hurt more. How could she dance to the Temptations when a Temptation is dead? She started to sing along as she so often did. But her singing was worse than usual. See, the Temptations made her feel she could sing, especially when she was alone with them. There isn't an oldies station in the land that can make it without the Temptations! Anytime there is a contest about the all-time favorites the Temptations take up a number of spots. She who owns so few records—and fewer compact discs—owns more Temptation albums than music of any other artist.

"Since I Lost My Baby" had never been long enough. Now it seemed it would never end. Eddie Kendricks is dead. And those "Temptin' Temptations" keep saying "Since I lost my baby.... feel so sad."

The national news could manage only ever so short clips of them singing. It seems they could have done a song, but, once again, she reminded herself that she was expecting too much. At least she heard that some stations played Temptations songs the whole weekend; that sounds right.

The song is still going. "...Everything is wrong; it's hard; it's hard to carry on." She hadn't known Kendricks had lung cancer. She didn't know he was ill. Did everyone know but her? The last time she saw him in Seattle he was as good as ever. She didn't know how many times she had seen the group. Maybe if she had known he was ill she would not have been so shocked.

When she had her annual oldies but goodies party every Labor Day Eve she always played more Temptations than any other artists. As she and the guests danced, they sang along. No one ever said, "Let's sing." People simply sang. They know all of the songs. One year two of the guys just started doing the very familiar Temptations routine. They had never done it together; they didn't talk about it. They simply did the whole thing as if they had practiced for years. Everybody applauded. What nobody said was that everybody could probably have done the steps minus any practicing.

At least the song finally ended. People die. Someone her age ought to know that truth by now. Get with it she told herself. Everybody knew how she was always urging all of the exercisers to keep at it, how they often said they couldn't keep up with her. No one could notice that she wasn't feeling up to being her cheerful self. In a few seconds the next song would begin....

Oh, no. Really now had this always been the order of the songs? She could not recall this being the case before. But today the second song was "Ain't Too Proud to Beg." This was amazing. She had always been swimming to two consecutive Temptations songs? She wondered if Atlas knew. She wondered if he thought about The Temptations, about Eddie Kendricks. She knew we had to go on. The song had never been so long.

Her sister had called long distance earlier. She wanted to make sure the *USA Today* article about Kendricks was sent to their brother—in prison. He loved the Temptations. This sister does not write him but wanted him to have the article. O.K. Of course. The article would be sent. At least *USA Today* thought Kendricks deserved a bit of space on a page.

"Ain't Too Proud to Beg" is still going. She recalled the article: "In November he lost a lung. 'But he came back kicking,' says [Tunis Wilson, his personal assistant]. We did the Apollo [Theater] in June, and I had a tank of oxygen at the side of the stage. He would get a whiff and keep performing. He never wanted to stop singing." At least the song ends.

The third tune cannot be one by the Temptations. It just couldn't be.

And it wasn't. The sound was that of "I Heard It Through the Grapevine." Groan, groan, groan. Marvin Gaye's death was as senseless as they come, more tragic than Kendricks' if there is a yardstick. She tried not to think about it. She could listen a long time without thinking about the two facts: his father killed him, and Marvin was only forty-five. "Grapevine" always seemed long. Now it was even longer. But finally it too ended.

She was ready for whatever came. But please, no more Temptations or Marvin Gaye.

It was as if someone were playing a terrible trick on her. It was her favorite Temptations song. It was the song that tops more all-time hit lists than any other. Is there anyone out there over thirty who does not know the first notes of "My Girl"? It's one of those songs that people liked immediately. It sounds so good. Maybe it is the water in the swimming pool that makes the sound more special than usual. "I've got sunshine on a cloudy day..." She actually plays games when the song comes on: how long can she listen without singing along? She had never gotten past "I don't need no money..." And here it was. And she had to sing. "I don't need no money, fortune or fame; I've got all the riches one man can claim..." She would not get out of this pool. Everybody exercising looked the same. Wasn't there someone besides her mourning the Temptations? She was sure this was the first time she had ever wanted "My Girl" to end quickly. But she did. She begged that it end. After what must have been the longest it has ever played, it ended.

———

And then she had to listen to Otis "Sitting on the Dock of the Bay." When Aretha came up with "Respect" she felt as if someone had removed a giant burden.

1992

The Phone Call

"Mrs. Cole? Is this Mrs. John Cole? M'am, I hate to tell you this. But there's been an accident. I have to give you some bad news. Your husband John—was killed."

The phone went dead. Meg shouldn't have been home. But she had gotten permission to come to work an hour late. She looked at the clock: 8:52 a.m. She could still get to work in time.

What was she thinking about? John had always teased her about the many absurd excuses she concocted so she could stay home: the cat had kittens last night; one of the flowers was dying; the goldfish died. No, she never stayed home. But she loved coming up with ideas, and he loved listening to her. Today she had fooled him. She hadn't given him an excuse. She smiled remembering. She was planning a surprise for his birthday. He would be fifty this weekend.

Immediately her thoughts went back to the phone call. She finally returned the phone to its cradle and sat down.

What had the man said? John was dead. God, how could he be dead? He had left home at 5:30 a.m. It wasn't 9:00 a.m. Then she smiled. He was always telling her in the most loving way, "Hon, one has nothing to do with the other."

They had the most wonderful relationship. She was thinking this; they never said it to each other. She had told him many, many times that he was the best something that had ever happened to her. And he had said the same to her—she was the best something that had ever happened to him. Although the two had been married more than twenty-seven years, countless friends teased them about acting like honeymooners. They really did not know any other way to act. Her stupid smile had returned. She had to stop smiling. All smiles had ceased for him.

What was she supposed to do? The kids, all four of them were at school. She would not go get them. She would keep this most horrible news from them for as long as she could. Besides, she had to determine what to say.

She hadn't asked what happened. The man certainly hadn't given any details. But he had said the worst he could say—except maybe one of the kids had been killed.

Where was John when it happened? How did it happen? Did he suffer? Where was he now?

She hadn't even gotten the name of the caller. She hadn't recognized his voice either. She did not know all of the guys, but she knew a few of them. Occasionally families of employers were invited to company outings.

John had at one time been one of the gang there. But for the past year or so, he and the fifteen to twenty men in his section, especially three of them, had grown apart. John was chief dispatcher. So he had the final say about who was hired.

For years everyone hired had been the son or brother or nephew or friend of someone who already worked there. But about seven years ago the company had come under new management. Gradually the man in charge had emphasized how more attention would be paid to the Equal Employment Opportunity signs prominently posted on walls throughout the building. The signs had been up at least a decade, but no one really noticed them anymore. No one really took the new manager seriously when he said, "We shall attempt in as many ways as possible to be fair. We're going to follow the rules. We're going to follow the affirmative action rules." There was no reason for anyone to think much of it. John had told her how the posters had begun to fade long before anyone ever mentioned adhering to them. It was as if no one actually expected anyone to make equality a reality. The only change had been the signs themselves.

Now why was she thinking about this? Only seventeen minutes had passed, yet it seemed like hours. She had been so peppy—she usually was, and John made her peppier. They really had a good life.

All of a sudden she was very sad that the trouble at the plant had been such a big worry during his last months. When John hired the first black about eight months ago, no one—not one—said anything to him about it, but the atmosphere changed. The employee was really quiet, and he did a wonderful job. But the coffee room, the working space—neither was ever the same. John did not talk about it often, but the few times he did talk, Meg knew him well enough to know that he spent lots of time thinking about the predicament.

John had not known precisely what to make of the situation. Oh, he knew several guys wanted no blacks on the job. He had never been in an environment that demanded his personal views about race; he knew nothing about his friends' feelings on the subject. But he soon learned that some of his friends were serious about not having blacks or anyone not white working in "their" area. Some of his co-workers thought it was enough that several blacks had been hired elsewhere in the company, so they themselves had not expected any changes in procedure in their totally white part of the work world. Two guys had relatives they wanted to have these very good-paying jobs. The great surprise came when the next two openings went to two more blacks. No one ever had a complaint about the black men's work, but the tension in the coffee room and on the dock worsened.

Finally Walt, a man John had known for at least twenty years, told John not to hire "anymore of those guys." Walt was not playing; this was not a joke. Although John knew Walt had not supported any of the three hirings, John was still startled when Walt told him not to hire anymore black individuals. Admittedly, John had never heard that particular tone in Walt's voice, but he decided to ignore Walt. The two men had been good friends for years. The fathers of both had worked at the plant until they retired. These sons started these jobs immediately after high school.

Called from her reverie, Meg knew she had better get to school. By now she had reasoned that having someone else tell the kids would be terrible. The news itself was terrible enough.

She considered calling someone to accompany her. But everyone was at work. Oh, she had to tell John's parents.

Maybe she could call the office and get more details before telling them. The parents, though septuagenarians, were very healthy. They were good in-laws.

But now she had to get to the school. Should she tell the eldest child first? By the time she got to the office, she had decided to get each child and tell them simultaneously. The four of them could comfort each other.

Almost an hour had passed, and she had said nothing to no one. As much as she thought she needed the details she decided she could get them later. The worst something had happened. Now she had to tell the kids and the parents.

Gretchen, some would say her dad's favorite, arrived at the office first. The calm, pretty-faced daughter knew her mom didn't come to the office without cause. Before Meg could say anything, Jim and Carlton arrived. Meg could see Becky skipping down the hall.

Wondering what John would do, Meg decided to take the kids home first but almost instantly realized she couldn't make the twenty-minute drive without telling them. She graciously accepted the principal's invitation to go into the small room adjoining his office. Without realizing it, she said exactly what the caller had said. She told her darlings their father was dead. The only positive something was not having to reveal this awful news four times and see the joys of her life hurt so terribly as she stood so helplessly.

"He can't be dead," said Gretchen the sensible teen-ager who worshipped her dad. She often said what could or couldn't be, and her dad always made the situation as she wanted it. Jim said nothing. His face looked like the clouds in The Wizard of Oz storm. It was the fifteen-year-old Mark who started to cry. His action seemed to tell the others crying was an appropriate action. Becky stood whimpering.

Eventually Meg managed to calm them enough to explain that she had to tell their grandparents. After checking to see that the couple was home, she and her kids made the long ride. She chose to leave the kids with the grandparents saying she had to get more details. Watching them and the kids was unbearable; having her children and these people who had been like ideal parents to her watch her was a pain she could no longer withstand.

The car seemed to return home automatically. Since the phone call, the day had been going so slowly despite the lightning-like movement of her mind. She sat there for what seemed like hours. Glancing at the clock, she dropped her head and sat staring at the chair where he usually sat. John would have been on his way home about now. She was never there when he arrived, but he always called her soon after he got inside the door. This daily call routine had begun long before they married. They had always believed one of them should be there when the kids got home. And they were among those fortunate parents who could make this belief an actuality. She sat on the slightly worn couch grateful that the kids couldn't see her giant tears, the first ones she had shed. She cried and cried.

About the time John would've been calling, the door opened. She heard it and did not hear it all at the same time. In walked John!

Expecting to see her because he had seen the car but knowing she shouldn't have been home, he ran straight to her. When she realized he was indeed there and not the product of her imagination, she cried more; she cried harder; she cried louder.

She told John what had happened. For only a few seconds was he baffled. He had indeed hired another black man, this morning, before nine. Walt was just the kind of person to execute such a heartless trick.

1992

Save Whom You Can

William Hanley's drama Slow Dance on the Killing Ground *isn't* a play I had heard of until a successful young actor told me that next to Cyrano, Hanley's protagonist Randall was his favorite part. For me, that was a more than ample endorsement. So I listened as he talked about the play with such passion that I had to read it.

Set in Brooklyn in a small store on the night of June 1, 1962, the play tells the story of an accidental meeting of a young black man named Randall who is determined to commit suicide and a German store owner Glas—with one "s"— who pretends he is Jewish although he escaped the Holocaust by abandoning his Jewish wife and child. In the midst of what gradually becomes a real conversation comes Rosie, a young white woman who had taken the wrong subway trying to find the site of her scheduled abortion. Their interactions make this a masterful piece of drama.

When I saw that the play would be performed locally, I reasoned that fate had smiled on me once again. A month ago I had not heard of the play; now I had read it, love it, and would get the chance to see it. As I expected, the performance was better than the reading. What struck me most was the line "Save who you can."

Randall had wanted to commit suicide, and Rosie was trying to convince him to do otherwise. Thinking about her planned abortion, he had yelled, "Leave me alone. Save who you can." In a number of ways that was a revelation to and for me. Saving everyone made sense, but the thought of doing so could easily dissipate one's energy. Realizing that I, nor no one else, can "save" everyone was something new. For years I had reminded others and myself that Jesus did not "save" everyone with whom He came in contact. Perhaps He could have, but He did not. Somehow this sentence made more of life make more sense to me. And it made life simpler too. Trying to save everyone can easily become all encompassing. Just thinking that at least someone out there believed we should try to save only those we could refreshed me. Yes, save whom you can. This was one of the epiphanies in my life.

I left the theater exhilarated—on a natural high—so much so that I did not go straight home but rather visited friends, one of those mismatched couples I enjoyed talking to, especially one or the other. You must know couples like them: you love him and you love her, but "they" can make you uncomfortable with their bickering which sometimes becomes open hostility. I had to talk to someone about the play, and they lived closest to the theater. I did not mind talking to him as I waited for her to come downstairs. In no time he and I were having one of our animated conversations, the play being its center. He asked a lot of questions, so I gave a lot of detail that I ordinarily would have skipped.

After a few minutes, however, I began to wonder what was keeping her although I did not mind talking to him. The continued discussion simply made me love the play more. But I knew she knew I was there, and although I had not called to say I was coming, I thought she could have come down. We do visit each other, neither of us making a point to call before visiting. Actually I had planned to stay only a few minutes; I had not planned to visit.

Perhaps feeling a bit uncomfortable and himself wondering where his wife was, he said he would get her. It seemed to have taken longer than it should have, but since I had not come as a result of an invitation, I had no complaint. Actually I had said he did not have to interrupt her. But he had insisted. I had just stopped by. She eventually came down; he had remained upstairs.

The expression on her face was not one of horror, but it definitely said she wasn't pleased with something or someone. It did not take too long for me to discover that I was the object of her anger. She was pregnant; this I knew. What I did not know was that she did not want the baby, that its conception, as with that of the child they now had and the abortion she had prior to that child, was what she called a mistake.

Before I showed up, they were having an intense discussion, actually an argument about whether she should have an abortion. He had "just about" agreed that she would have one. Then the doorbell rang.

I came in. She had left the room because she did not wish to talk to anyone. I had told him about the play. He had come upstairs to get her. He had also taken the time to remind her that she had had one abortion. This baby should not be aborted. No, it would not be aborted. They would have this baby. "And it's your fault," she said.

1992

Through the Other's Eyes

Finally Sandy was coming. For at least twenty years Joy had tried her best to get her Louisiana friend to visit her in Seattle. They had met in second grade more than thirty years ago. Both had endured much. They talked on the phone several times a year. And Joy always called on Sandy's birthday. Sandy too would call; they would talk an hour or so; they would hang up; the other would call back; they would talk another hour or so. They wrote letters. Among the letters Joy had kept was a seventeen-page one Sandy wrote years ago. Once when Joy had visited Sandy the two had had a long talk about Joy's diminishing faith, Sandy had sent a card that reads, "I had a long talk with God about you last night." The inside said, "I think I got you out of trouble." Something reminds Joy of the card several times a year, but Sandy doesn't remember sending it. But it's ok; Joy has the card. Sandy has laughed about it on the rare occasions Joy has told her about it, but Sandy still doesn't remember it. Joy thinks that is funny in a weird way. And she can't understand why Sandy doesn't remember; Sandy has a good memory. But the card is Joy's concrete proof that the card-sending took place. Joy has the card—on her spare bedroom wall. The two women share heavy-duty secrets. One can call the other any time and with very little—if any—introduction, pick up a thread of a long-completed conversation and talk for hours.

Why had it taken Sandy so long to make the trip? Joy regularly extended the invitation, and whenever she visited home, she always visited Sandy or if she did not have access to a car, Sandy visited her. Sandy is only one of two persons Joy has seen on every one of her trips there in the past twenty-three years. Joy never abandoned her desire to get her friend to visit the beautiful Seattle. Actually, Joy was always trying to get everybody to visit Seattle. She couldn't imagine how someone who had the wherewithal to visit Seattle would not have visited. Joy always talked about the beautiful mountains and how the definition of flat should be Louisiana.

For some reason, Joy decided not to ask Sandy to visit this time. She simply sent Sandy an airline coupon in the mail. And after one brief phone call, Sandy had purchased a ticket!

Another former second-grade classmate, Shelly, and Joy picked up Sandy at the airport. All three talked at the same time. No one could have guessed that the three of them had not been together since the 1963 high-school graduation. The conversations covered years past, but the closeness seemed never to have left. The women were girls again, high school maybe. The glee seemed to be self-perpetuating. Shelly, who had almost as many plans for Sandy as Joy had, couldn't wait for Sandy to spend the night at her house. She had already invited friends to come on the night Sandy arrived.

Although Joy had recently had surgery and was somewhat restricted, she felt certain Sandy's presence would make her feel better fast. They spent most of the night talking. There were the families, the classmates, the other friends at home and elsewhere.

Then on Friday, Joy had an ice cream party for Sandy. Thirteen others who had attended the same high school attended. Hugs and kisses took up most of the time. The rarity of such euphoria escaped not one of the participants.

Everything was perfect until one of the men wanted to know what Sandy thought of the Space Needle. When she said she hadn't been, several wanted to know why Joy had not taken her there. Never had it occurred to anyone that Sandy had refused to go. Joy calmly admitted that she had indeed tried more than once to take Sandy but had been told Sandy was not interested. Sandy said she had seen the Space Needle as they drove by and that was sufficient. Although Joy shared their astonishment, she did not join the ones who spoke as if some crime had been committed because Sandy was here in Seattle but would not go to the top of the Needle. Joy had been betting that once the group talked about the Space Needle, Sandy would change her mind. No, Sandy reiterated; she did not want to go. When the discussion stayed on the Needle, Sandy finally blurted that she was afraid of heights!

Questioned one of the males, "Did you fly out here?"

When Sandy answered "yes," everyone knew she would see the "logic" of going to the Space Needle.

But her logic worked differently. Despite the number of times the subject had arisen—or rather Joy or someone else had resurrected it—now, for the first time, Joy sadly but clearly realized that Sandy had no intention of going to the top of the Space Needle.

A certain calmness came over the group for a short time, but soon the noise level ascended. By the time everyone had gone, the two friends were ready for a well-deserved rest.

The next day Shelly had made reservations at a restaurant of an ilk one would never find in our hometown. Joy herself had been there only once. With absolutely no hesitation, Sandy said she did not wish to go. Shelly's voice revealed her disappointment. So when she said she would be over shortly, Joy knew Shelly was coming to convince Sandy to go.

Sure enough, Shelly arrived. Any stranger could see her great spirits. Shelly described the place in detail and for a short time made the sick Joy herself consider reconsidering accompanying them. But again, without the slightest hesitation, Sandy said she did not want to go. Shelly could not understand. Perhaps if Sandy had said she was ill or tired or sleepy, Shelly could have accepted her response, but Sandy said only that she did not wish to go.

From that point the tenor of the reunion changed. Nobody said it, but the three friends knew it. The Space Needle was not mentioned, but the three of them were thinking about it; no, they were thinking about Sandy's not visiting it. The Space Needle and now the restaurant—or, at least her not going—had done something that the years of physical separation had not done.

Sandy and Shelly jogged and rode horses. Sandy and Joy saw plays and went shopping. Sandy spent a night with an elderly friend. She talked to many friends on the phone. The three classmates went to church.

Then two days before Sandy was to leave she declined another invitation from Shelly for another outing that she and Joy knew was not possible in their hometown. Joy, of course, could not understand why. All she could see was that Sandy had the opportunity to do something she had not done before, something she could never do at home. Joy had done it many times but was gladly willing to do it again only because she wanted Sandy to do it.

When Sandy said no, Joy exploded, "I am trying so hard with you."

Without averting her eyes, Sandy immediately responded, "I am trying hard with you too."

Anyone who had witnessed this ever so short incident would have known how sincere the two women were about their very different perspectives. After a very long pause, the two looked at each other. It was no doubt that they also looked at the situation. Neither ever mentioned the Space Needle again. And five years later, they still don't.

1992

The Turkish Rug Factory

The exhilaration I felt while touring ancient Ephesus did not prepare me for my visit to a Turkish carpet factory. For a while I had no idea where the tour group was going. The guide kept referring to "the demonstration." And since I wouldn't think of missing part of a prepaid tour, I casually walked along.

As the group of French, Australians, New Zealanders, and Americans waited to cross the street, the Turk guide said in impeccable English, "We will now visit a carpet factory." Because I had been very disappointed tapestry makers were on vacation while I was in Belgium, I took this visit as the perfect opportunity to learn information which would probably be of no benefit to me but, nevertheless, interesting, fascinating, and educational.

Saying he had little expertise in carpet-making, our tour guide introduced us to an expert. We ten tourists were ushered into a room and invited to sit down on three benches that lined three walls. On the fourth wall were at least fifty carpets of various sizes. Each was neatly rolled. Several young men were milling around. The new guide asked if we wanted coffee, tea, or something cold to drink. Shortly thereafter in came a young man with ten orange drinks at no cost to us.

The expert began by telling us that nobody knows how long ago the first rug was made but it was made in Turkey. Girls were and are taught this art by their mothers. However, the girls make carpets not for money but because a prospective husband can know a woman by her work only. A man who visits a Turkish home never sees an unmarried girl: the girl goes to her room. He knows an unmarried girl is in a house by the presence of a bottle on a chimney: two bottles, for example, indicate two virgins. A cracked bottle indicates a married woman. A scarf hanging on a door also says an unmarried girl is a resident of a particular house. How handicrafts are made is still another way a man knows a virgin is in a house: fringe around a rug made by a virgin is knotted; fringe around a rug made by a married woman is loose. A male visitor would know an unmarried girl lives in a house simply because of the signs, not because he saw the girl. "There's no romance in Turkey," said the guide.

Two men brought in a loom. A woman who looked to be in her mid-thirties came in, got on her knees on a beautiful Turkish rug, and began to weave on a rug that was approximately eight inches high and five feet wide. She worked extremely fast—several tourists commented. We guests were amazed at how deftly her hands moved. Then the guide asked her to weave at a "normal" rate. Her hands still moved very fast, we thought. Girls all over Turkey do this work. They do not weave with a pattern.

Their mothers taught them how to make the pattern in the carpet. They will teach it to their daughters. The women hold a knife as they weave, but do not use it to cut the yarn; they use their fingernails for this purpose. They have no tape measure because they know how long a piece of yarn should be. They have nothing to indicate which piece of yarn to weave next. They know which naturally dyed strand to use and when. They know how many strands to pull and where. They know that they must tie 380 knots per square inch in some carpets but 680 knots per square inch in silk carpets.

The expert seemed to be so proud that every phase of the carpet-making is done by hand. A machine could be used, but the carpets would not be as soft, he said. A particular design is indigenous to a particular region. Some rug patterns are quite scarce. The girls and women can work only three to five hours a day. Married women must do other chores and take care of their children and their husbands. A girl can work on silk only two years of her life. Work of this kind can definitely lead to blindness if done too many years. This woman has made rugs thirty-two years!

The presentation continued as we were shown rug after rug. There are rugs for praying. There are rugs for hanging. There are rugs for the floor. The rugs keep the houses warm, and in Turkey the temperature can be as low as fifteen degrees. The rugs feel good to the touch. The expert assured us, "All of the tiredness seems to leave when a person steps on the rug." Perhaps Turks are "unfamiliar" with rheumatism because when they enter their houses they pull off their shoes and walk on these quality-made rugs, these rugs not made for money. There are various colors from which to choose, either the natural color of the wool or colors dyed with fruits, vegetables, or tree roots: greens, blues, reds, oranges, beige. There are rugs made of wool, wool and cotton, and silk. There are rugs with a medallion in the center and rugs with a tree of life in the center. The tree of life rugs have steps to paradise at the top and a water pot on either side at the bottom. The spiel was perfect.

As we attentively listened, young men steadily lay all sizes and colors of beautiful rugs before us. On occasion we were encouraged to feel the rugs. "Take your shoes off and walk on the rugs." This is the only way, we were told, we could feel the quality. Finally the expert announced, "Just before my presentation is over, I want to give you an idea about the prices. When a rug is lifted from the floor, just indicate that you're interested. One of my friends—all speak well (sic) English—will come over to help you."

After hearing how early the girls begin working and how long this woman has worked, I began wondering how she felt. The guide assured us that the industry is giving women a larger share of the money. "Women have a hard life in Turkey," he said.

As the rugs were lifted, my fellow tourists often showed their interest: a raised hand, a sigh, a "how much." Always the guide had that rug put in front of the questioning party. Some people had five or six in front of them. The guide's friends took some tourists to other rooms so they could "see the rugs on the floor." Other tourists were assisted where they sat. Looking rather repulsed, one lady thanked the guide and left. I just sat. A carpet factory worker was helping everyone.

As I got up, someone came to help me choose a rug. He asked if I liked the rugs. I said I did and explained I could not afford one. Talking to him and not talking to him at the same time, I said, "The price is extremely high." With a beautiful smile, he attempted to assure me that I could definitely afford a rug. When I repeated that I could not, he asked me to wait a minute. He then got a smaller rug, a size that had not been shown. He could let me have it for $130.00. I could have a silk one for $1200.00. I could charge it, he said.

Still thinking about the weaver, I said I would like to talk to the woman who was weaving. He led me to the room where she sat intently spinning wool. The loom was behind her. She did not speak English, but one of the men asked another to translate for me. The men were very helpful. I wanted to know how the woman felt about her job. Without translating what I had said, he asked me how I felt about my job. I told him that I loved teaching, I had chosen to teach. "But," I asked, "Would you please ask her how she feels?" He said he did not speak very good English. I pointed out that his English is much better than my Turkish and asked again that he tell her what I had said.

By now she had motioned for me to sit on the floor next to her. As I sat, I asked him again to translate for me. He did. Pointing to the eight-inch height of the unfinished carpet, she said, he told me, "I feel very low, about this high." Before he could finish translating, she grabbed my hand very firmly. I then asked him to ask her what would she have been if she could have chosen. But before he could translate for me, she gripped my hand more firmly and pulled me closer. He told me she had said that she would like to have been a singer. She clung to my hand in such a way that I am positive no one had ever asked her that question. Perhaps no one had ever thought of asking her that question.

Someone called the salesman.

The woman's small son came and sat next to us. I asked how many children she has. She held up four fingers. I could tell she wanted to ask me the same question, so I told her that I have no children. Another salesman joined the conversation telling me that she had two girls and two boys. I asked him to ask her if her daughters were being trained to make rugs. "Of course," he said, without asking her.

"Suppose," said I, "they would like to be singers as she would like to have been."

The salesman who had told me he was a "relation" of the woman, the same salesman who had tried to sell me the rug, asked if I wanted a rug. "This is a business," he said. He could let me have the rug for $110.00. I did not have to pay until December. "We trust Americans. Americans are good people." The woman and I held hands for a very long moment.

I left the factory certain that I had been right earlier when I told the expert that I could not afford the carpet. I still wonder if he will ever know how expensive those carpets not made for money really cost.

1985

What the Kids Learn

For as far back—no, for a long time I have been twenty-three. I don't recall when I decided to be twenty-three, but it must have been during the time I was twenty-three, because I do not remember being twenty-four or twenty-five. And I certainly do not know about thirty-something! A psychologist might explain my phenomenon by saying because I was five when I started to school and it seemed EVERYBODY was six or seven—I developed a complex about age. Of course, I would disagree. I do know that EVERYBODY was a teen-ager before I was! And, oh, when they all became sixteen.... Of course, by the time we were twenty-one, we were all over the country, but I still remember the birthdates of a rather large number of my classmates and make a point of calling or sending cards.

There is something about being twenty-three, something which I cannot explain. But twenty-three felt/feels good. I simply like twenty-three. Perhaps there is no special reason. I have tried to come up with one good reason, and I can't. I do know that when I was twenty-three my mom was alive although not as well as I naively believed she was and although we lived more than 2000 miles apart, we continued to have what I eventually came to realize was a very good relationship. I was single, out of school, working. It was a good time.

It seems I just started saying I was twenty-three. The nieces and the nephews rarely questioned me. On occasion one would say, "Auntie, I thought you were twenty-three last year." I'd say I was and keep the conversation going—on another subject. Once one said, "I thought you were older than Mom." I assured him that once upon a time I had been older, but not anymore.

But there's one nephew—isn't there always one? He asked more questions than anyone. A few years ago, he called me long distance. "Auntie, how old is Christopher [another nephew]?"

"Twenty-one."

"I thought so. Didn't you put diapers on him?"

"Of course, I have diapered all of my nephews."

"Well, if Cousin Chris is twenty-one and you are twenty-three, you were only two when you were putting diapers on him."

With not even the hint of a pause in the conversation, I replied, "Yes, Baby. Auntie has been working hard all of her life."

This was the closest call I had ever had.

One day, I called my sister. This same little smart nephew answered. He was twelve then. When he said his mom was not there, I asked when would she return. He said, "She and Dad are in South America."

Of course, I immediately remembered. Knowing a number of aunts and uncles live near them, I wanted to know who was there with him and his older brother. He said no one. I told him that I knew better. In his most playful voice, he said, "No, we are here alone."

"I know my sister would not leave you alone."

"Auntie, I am sixteen. My brother and I can stay alone."

Amazed, I replied, "Little nephew, you are not sixteen."

"Yes, I am."

"Nephew, this is Auntie. I was there the day you were born. I know how old you are."

"No, really, Auntie, I am sixteen."

"Boy, I know you are twelve!"

"Auntie, you are twenty-three; I am sixteen."

1988

Inauguration Day

She woke up feeling good. Actually, she usually wakes up feeling good. A number of friends chide her about being so cheerful so early and so often. Most of the time she doesn't think about whether she is or isn't cheerful. She simply gets up and gets on with the tasks of the day. Although a terrible storm was brewing, according to the weatherman, she knew this morning was different. She herself noted she felt good. This was Inauguration Day 1993.

How many Inauguration Days she had endured? She didn't know and didn't care to count. But she knew for a fact that she had never ever felt this way.

Before getting out of bed she relived the television show from the previous night. Because of another outing, she had taped the program. She had arrived home in the midst of Aretha singing as only Aretha can sing. Although the song wasn't familiar, Joy sensed something about Aretha's singing that made Joy want to do nothing but listen. So she did. Other entertainers made their contributions. And there were quite a few: Although blacks complain that more blacks are not visible in government, no one could say blacks were not represented at the gala. Goldie Hawn's narrative about her deceased father and how she wished he were present touched Joy in a way only someone who has lost a beloved parent can be touched.

The disc jockey said more than once the station would broadcast the "coronation." This was Joy's cue to set the tape. She put in an eight-hour one; she wanted to see it all! She did have to go to work.

As she rushed through the daily ritual of getting ready, she was preoccupied with inauguration—actually with the campaign, the election. Glimpses of much of the campaign, especially the last few months, crossed her mind. One friend had said she was leaving the country if Bush won. Another very good friend had said she was leaving the country if Clinton won. Furthermore, this person had presented a decent argument for voting for Perot and then tried to convince Joy to do the same. Joy's answer that she was voting for Clinton made friend Marty respond: "You can't possibly vote for Clinton! He shows his disrespect for blacks by selecting a white Southerner as a running mate. He is ignoring us!" There was more, but Joy kept quiet, knowing there are those conversations which end although the parties keep talking. Besides, this was not the time for Joy to tell her friend that she believed the President responsible for the greatest gains since the signing of the Emancipation Proclamation was a white Southerner—Lyndon Baines Johnson. Maybe he had not had the vision to suggest the changes; perhaps he did not want all of them, but he had enough clout—or debts outstanding—to make the Civil Rights Act a reality. Joy concluded Clinton would do the same. He understood the South as no Northerner could.

There was no reason to think about this now. She skipped to the car where she heard more talk about the Inauguration. The good feeling was higher now. She could talk to the two carpoolers about the day. It seemed that all three were in good moods. As Joy chatted about the day, she surprised herself by saying she wished she could be there, in Washington, D.C. Had she really said that? Yes, and she meant it. She wished that she could be in D.C. She wanted to be part of the atmosphere. What was she saying? So she had never said it; she had never thought about going to an inauguration, but now she was saying she wanted to be there. She had come a long way! One rider pragmatically and practically pointed out that she probably couldn't get into any of the affairs. The other understood that Joy did not have to think about whether she could get in; she simply wanted to be there. The good feeling edged upward.

By the time they had made the thirty-two-mile drive, Joy was higher still. In her office building were others—at least the ones she saw—who seemed to feel as she did. One man who in all the years she had known him had never ever seemed happy on this day appeared as high as Joy.

Giving a test to a class consisting of a number of people who were obviously not prepared failed to lower her spirits—as such a happening usually did. When fewer than half of the students did not come to the second class—ostensibly because of the storm—she had class as if everyone were present. A number of incidents worked to make the third class's visit to the computer laboratory a disaster, but she continued to smile, told the students she was determined to have a good day. When she said that, she had forgotten the deep cleaning scheduled at the periodontist's.

During the drive home, both driver and rider mentioned events which ordinarily would have been disturbing, but not today. A chat with the friendly receptionist who commented that Joy was always in a good mood got the comment that she had voted for Clinton. The receptionist volunteered that she hadn't—her parents and siblings, grandmother too, all had voted for him, but she had not and still could not see his winning as something positive. Joy assured her that it was ok, that she would see. Though everyone had warned how terribly painful such a procedure is, Joy emerged from the anesthetic feeling fine. The lower left of her mouth was still dead, but there was no pain. A chat with the hygienist—who had voted for Clinton—kept the good feeling in the air.

Finally, at home she made a discovery she had thought about—the storm had knocked out the cable! All of her taping had come to nought. Well, she reasoned, "I'll catch Dan Rather's news." What had not crossed her mind was the medication in her system. She went to sleep although she had gotten in bed to read the paper. She woke up at exactly 6:30 p. m.—the time Rather goes off! She laughed out loud. Ok, she concluded, "I'll see it at 11:00 p.m."

In a few hours there would be a special "48 Hours"; its subject was BEHIND the Inauguration. For someone who wanted so much to see "the" Inauguration, she was having a hard time. As she waited, she did talk to a few folks on the telephone. A black person from Indiana, quite a few years older than Joy, admitted that she too felt about this Inauguration as she had never felt about another one. A younger, white friend in Texas expressed the same kind of feeling.

She was not alone with her good feelings. Knowing that others felt the same way increased her pleasure. For one who had seen so little of the festivities, she was certainly having a wonderful day. All she had to do was be patient. Access to cable ensured her seeing such happenings. Switching from channel to channel, catching one inaugural ball after another, she couldn't believe she couldn't find the ceremony itself. This occasioned more laughter. Again she expressed her gratitude to her God. More than ever before she felt Americans had another opportunity to make the oft quoted words of the Declaration of Independence and Constitution a reality, a reality for all Americans, not simply white males who owned property. Sometimes she was sorry she knew so much about the origin of these documents and the men who formulated them, but this knowledge did not sadden her tonight.

With the clock approaching midnight, she changed channels one more time. Ted Koppel! Why hadn't she remembered him? He must have some great pictures. With the show already in progress, she heard Koppel say, "To my two words, you answer with one. President Clinton." Several people made comments, comments that might not have been Joy's but did echo her voice.

And then there was Koppel repeating his question. This time the listener was an older white man, fifty-five, maybe sixty. He couldn't have known how happy Joy had been all day. He couldn't have been thinking about her; he certainly did not know her. But he said, "I can't say this on tv."

Koppel assured him he could, "It's late. Go ahead."

Slightly hesitating, the man said, "He's too much for blacks."

All of the euphoria which had surrounded her all day vanished in an instant. Had he really said that? Here she was being stupid again. Yes, she had heard correctly. The man had said not the obscenity she and probably Koppel had expected. He had made a sentence that to her was much worse: "He is too much for blacks."

She tried to make the smile come back. She wanted it to come as easily as it had come all day, but it would not come. She told herself that this was the remark of only one man; all of the other opinions had been positive. This was one opinion. Yet even as she said that she knew it was not one opinion only. Oh, it was one opinion on that show that night. But there are others of the same opinion. She herself had realized that Clinton appeared to be distancing himself from blacks during the campaign. She had to admit that some Republicans on television tonight had said that what they wanted for Clinton was four years, that others had said Bush had done great things and history would say so. None of this had been able to destroy that good feeling. But this man, this little man had wiped her out with, "He's too much for blacks." She was ashamed she had let him spoil her joy, but he had. She turned out the light. Maybe there had been a reason she had not seen the Inauguration although she had tried good-naturedly to do so.

1993

Make the Cops Burn Rubber

"...Make the cops burn rubber" Nike.

What had the man said? Perhaps I had misunderstood. Then he repeated his question: "The billboard said, 'Make the cops burn rubber. Nike.' It's down now. Somebody protested, and it's down now. I just wondered if you would comment."

"That's materialism. We have to teach our children not to be materialistic. We have to let them know that all this emphasis on clothes and shoes is wrong," the esteemed speaker for the scholarship luncheon replied as several hundred people—definitely not wearing Nikes today—listened intently.

My mind was whirling. Had I heard what I thought I heard? I had reluctantly come to a 1:00 p.m. Saturday luncheon; I hate Saturday luncheons. But my good friend had told me the speaker is "good, very good." Since I had heard of him but never heard him, I concluded that I should go. My friend would be happy; the scholarship fund would be increased by twenty dollars; I wouldn't have to look for dinner, and I would hear a "good, very good" speaker.

As I said, my friend was very happy. The scholarship fund got its money. I would still have to look for dinner. But the speech "Making a Difference: Education for the 21st Century" had been better than average. The anecdotes were good and appropriate. It makes sense "to know, care, and act," to lift as we climb," (Mary McLeod Bethune), and to "be ashamed to die until you've won some victory for humankind" (Horace Mann). I considered myself a victor. Actually I was trying to find an unobtrusive way to leave. Because I was already late for a three o'clock meeting, I had decided to listen to only one question from the audience and then make my exit. Well, I had heard a question. Worse, I had heard an answer. By now I had forgotten about leaving.

The question pounded my brain, but then the speaker's answer worsened the pounding. I quietly asked someone to ask the questioner where this billboard had been. His response "Rainier Valley" did anything but calm me even as I was sure there was no place for such a billboard. The audience knows Rainier Valley—predominately black, often referred to as the most integrated area in Seattle. At least two women at my table of eight appeared to be as frustrated as I was. Our brief comments displayed our rudeness as others proceeded to ask questions on very different subjects. "He didn't answer the question," said the mother whose thirty-year-old daughter animatedly agreed. Alternating between being upset by the contents of the billboard and the speaker's response brought on a headache. Someone else asked another question. This was my cue to vacate the premises.

I hurried to the car thinking first about the comment and then about the answer. Neither refusing to believe what I had heard nor trying not to think about what I had heard worked. Couldn't this man see that the billboard commented on much more than materialism? Didn't he see the billboard made an assumption about the people in Rainier Valley? Residents break laws. Thus, residents are always running from cops. Nikes would make residents run faster. The cops would have to run faster still—burn more rubber—to catch the lawbreakers. Surely there was at least another way to explain the meaning of the billboard. How could the speaker be intelligent if all he saw was materialism? Of course, he is right about the materialism and the tremendous value too many of us place on it. But doesn't he see that some of us would probably place less value on objects if we had a society that teaches us differently? Can't he see the connection between how many people, especially youngsters, value themselves by their ownership of Nikes? I had wanted to question the questioner more. Maybe he could have given me answers that would have reduced or possibly eliminated this ache in my head. Perhaps he had misread. Could Nike or any other company make something good from "Make the cops burn rubber"?

The twenty-minute drive to the next meeting did not diminish the many disturbing thoughts. Sitting in the meeting diligently trying to listen to the business of the moment took more energy than I had. It was as if I were viewing the billboard through various lenses: 35mm to 70mm to 90mm and back again and not always in that order. Even as I joined the meeting discussion, I continued to think about the billboard.

Finally, I told the group of African-American writers what I had heard about the billboard, the question, responses. Although we did not talk about the sentence, some visual responses were similar to mine. One person said we should not let the billboard's coming down be the end. Another just shook his head in disgust.

I had to find the billboard. I was sorry I had gotten us off the subject but glad to know more than the woman, her daughter, and I were the only persons who objected to the sentence. I had to be sure that some information was missing. We got back to the business of the meeting.

A short time later, member Michael suggested that each of the dozen or so of us write on the sentence "Make the cops burn rubber." We could approach it as we chose. So, he too, had been thinking about the sentence. Only one person, senior member Ruby, protested. Noting the glee with which the group responded to Michael's suggestion, she said we might not want to write on that subject, we might be giving young people the wrong message. I could not understand how we could give the wrong message. And at this time I had more to say to the ones responsible for the billboard. I never want anyone burning rubber—not if it means running or driving in an unlawful manner to arrest kids or anyone else. Another member believed that Ruby and I were saying the same.

Though I was disappointed and dismayed, I could see how someone could make such a statement. What I could not see was how such a statement could pass through all the hands I assumed it would have to pass through and no one see its insensitivity and error. I could not see how anyone could see anything positive about it.

The meeting progressed, but my mind stayed in the same place. As soon as we adjourned, I approached Ruby. I was anxious to know how this sentence could be positive. She said again that she was neutral; she saw the sentence neither positively nor negatively. She reminded me that I had not seen the picture accompanying the advertisement. She could not think of an interpretation for the sentence.

The sentence continued to preoccupy my thoughts Saturday night and much of Sunday. Monday morning I awakened thinking about the ad. Thumbing through newspapers, as I often do, I saw a three-month old article in "Pacific Northwest Magazine," a section of the *Seattle Post-Intelligencer*; Nike was the subject. The Saturday incident was boldly back on my mind! I read with great interest about the advertising agency which creates Nike commercials.

And then I called a billboard company. Yes, Nike is a customer. No, the sales representative remembered no such sign. Someone would get back to me with information as soon as possible. For the first time, I think I completely forgot about the sentence.

In less than an hour, the phone rang. The billboard sales representative had instructed someone to call and give me the information I wanted. I explained. The director of communications knew nothing about a protest although the sign had been taken down. She had found an ad that I was most likely referring to. She would mail a copy.

The next day a photograph of the billboard arrived. A picture of a right foot wearing an "Air Pegasus" and showing the Nike swoosh has written beneath it "Get 1,500 Cops To Burn Rubber." And beneath this sentence in smaller type is "The Special Olympics Law Enforcement Run. 1-800-752-7559."

———

First, I was glad Nike had not written the ad as the man had described it. Second, I wanted to tell the man who asked the question and stop him from asking this question elsewhere. I am sure he didn't see the billboard. Then I wanted to tell everyone at the luncheon, especially those who may have seen and heard what I saw and heard. Next the group came to mind. I had imagined what several members had done with "Make the cops burn rubber": Michael a syncopated rap, full of anger; Bernard a shorter, slower rhythm but equally intense denouncement; Mr. Alexander a two-to-three-page essay about the idiocy of Nike and others who take our money while giving us little in exchange. I hoped that everyone had written something on the subject. I wanted to hear what they had thought and then what they had said. Had the sentence occupied as much of their thought space as it had mine? I certainly hoped not. What could they have been doing rather than writing about this sentence?

I'm very glad that I have a copy of the ad. I'll make a point of telling every one I know about it as it appeared. I'll show it to everyone at the meeting.

What distresses me most is the amount of energy spent as a result of someone's misquote. How many others will hear this misquoted sentence? How many will spend energy tracking it down, or, worse, not tracking it down but spreading it? How long will those of us who have been battered so much continue to expect to be battered? (It takes so much energy and time to be on guard all of the time.)

1992

Leaving

He was leaving—it wasn't midnight, and he wouldn't be on a train to Georgia. But his leaving was definite.

He had loved her so much. Everybody knew it. The two of them were one of those couples who walk down the street and everybody knows the two of them are in love. He looked at her with one of those looks that any sane body could read. That man loved that woman. That's probably why she had hurt him so terribly, not intentionally she would probably argue. This was just the way she was would say some of those who know her best.

He and she had met through work. She was interested in getting the job he was vacating. After putting in her application but before the interview, she had been bold enough to call him and ask specifically what his boss wanted. He had been impressed by her directness. That's why he had told her everything she wanted to know as well as additional information which could assist her.

A few weeks later, when she had the job, she called him to let him know. It was then that he said, I gave you vital information. You owe me a drink." She had laughed—and loud too. Now, she told him, she had wondered if he were black, but now he removed all doubt. It was his turn to laugh.

Because she was slightly past being jilted and he had lost a hardly fought battle against a divorce, both were as free as most humans can be.

He liked everything about her—well, everything except her use of time: when she felt the need to be on time, she was; when she did not feel the need, she wasn't. And she could take hours to get to her destination. Most of her friends had stories about how they had waited for her a long time. He often told the story of his longest wait—2½ hours on a street corner. He, like the friends, had always concluded she had a really good reason for being so late. And she could be so apologetic—that is when she believed she was late. She was good at saying, "No, we were supposed to meet at ____" whatever time she arrived. Telling her differently or showing her an appointment meant nothing. Usually people were so glad she had finally arrived that they didn't fuss too much, at least not to her.

Oh, but he loved her company. They could talk all night long. Seriously, she had everything he thought a partner for himself should have: education, goals, determination, and she had communication skills unmatched by anyone he knew. And she had more; she had grace and style. The fringe benefit was her beauty. She had the look that so many men wanted their dates to have.

It did not take long for them to become serious. All of their talking made the situation ideal. He was doing so much he had not done prior to his first marriage. So they had a fabulous wedding, definitely storybook, fairy tale. They traveled. They did all of those things real people do; there was nothing fake about their happiness. He had never been so happy; he had no idea he could be so happy.

After several years, she had begun to talk about having a baby although they had agreed before the marriage not to have children. Convincing him to change his mind took more time than she had ever guessed, but she eventually convinced him. The logic used the years before marriage was no longer apropos, she argued. He was wrong. She certainly remembered that he had two children, a boy and a girl. She even cried when he told her how futilely he had tried to prevent his first wife Charlesetta from having an abortion. But she calmly, logically argued, "I don't have a child." Years later he would tell their friends how he had used this as a point not to marry: he had a boy and a girl; she had no children; she needed to find someone who wanted children.

Saying "You didn't have a child when you agreed we would have no children" helped his case not at all. Adding that he knew she was too busy to be the kind of mother he thought she should be was of no help either. She knew she would be a good mother, she said; just let her prove it.

Two years later—after having had a beautiful baby—he was reminding her that he had been right, she was not what they had decided was a good mother. She had refused to change her busy schedule. She had little time for the baby. But he loved his wife more than ever. He loved their house, their home. He loved the baby. Not a dad who refers to himself as a babysitter, he spent lots of time with the baby, all kinds of time the military had prevented him from spending with the other children. He disagreed with her theories about quality time—for him, all time should be quality. He no longer mentioned this difference. She needed to get out, to keep her busy pace. He told himself he understood.

What he did not know was that even when she was supposed to be with the baby, she had often dropped the baby off at a sitter's. What he didn't know couldn't hurt him, she reasoned. But he did go out with her less. He talked to her less. He watched television more. And he watched alone more.

When she mentioned a second baby, he exploded. How dare she! Using the ammunition mustered from what he termed her poor parenting, he wanted to discuss nothing. No! No. He could handle one baby; he was doing a good job she and her friends agreed, some wishing their husbands helped at least half as much. He could not, would not handle two babies. She would not change. She may not have known it, but he knew it, regardless of what she said. He loved her, and he loved the baby, but there would be no Baby Two. Their biggest argument, maybe their only real argument, was having a second child. This argument would not die. She brought up the subject ever so often; the end was always the same—she wanted a baby; he did not want a baby. He tired of the subject. He moved from their bedroom.

For at least a year, he slept downstairs, and she slept in what had been their wonderful bedroom. Only the two of them knew what had—or hadn't—happened. Whenever anyone saw them, they were still the beautiful couple they had always been. Arm wrapped around his arm, she looked gorgeous. He felt proud as they ventured out.

One night she decided to break the silence. After a perfumed bath, she dressed in the most luxurious manner, a manner to which he had long become accustomed but had not witnessed in months. Descending the stairs like the African queen she could have been, she went to him, apologized profusely, explained he was right, of course, he was. As much as she did not want an only child, she thanked God that his other two children are sister and brother to their one child; it is not as if they have no contact with his third child. Yes, he was right. Finally, she accepted his argument.

Their detailed talk was like old times. He confessed he detested the discord, but he knew he was right, and he was glad she had come to accept his conclusion. Clearly, he loved her and the baby but no more babies. He believed with every fiber of his being that he was right. Absolutely nothing was to be gained from talking about babies. He was adamant, sorry she was saddened by this decision, but adamant, nevertheless. It took a few minutes before he realized she agreed with him. Silly man, she had come downstairs to tell him she agreed. They must get past this terrible rift, they could do it, they loved each other. There would be no babies.

Although she was seductively dressed, he had not considered "making love." Not having a baby was serious business. He was a serious man about such a serious subject. He knew he had made the right choice. He was glad she had finally seen his was the only decision they could sensibly make. He was glad they had passed that deadlock—a year was a long time to live as they had lived. It was particularly hard when to everyone who knew them "knew" how happy they were. Many, many times she had not wanted to do this, but he honestly knew of no other way to cope with the problem.

So when she approached him, he was cautious. The past year of not being intimate, not even speaking to each other in the house could not be cast aside after this good talk. And it had been a good talk. Still he took a chance of renewing the argument. Afraid he would insult her or at least hurt her feelings, he, nevertheless, felt he had to ask her if she were sure this was what she wanted. He knew what he wanted; he wanted her badly but only if she could not get pregnant. Nothing could make him change his mind. He would not spend a few minutes, or a night, only to regret that time for all time, and he was certain he would. So, clumsily he asked. "Do you have on the diaphragm?"

Startled, she moved closer and kissed him. He pushed her away—gently, but still he pushed her away.

"What do you think?" she asked.

After a bit of foreplay, he asked again about the diaphragm. As honest as ever, she said she was prepared. It did not take him long to relax. He even felt the need to apologize for questioning her. He should have known she had on the diaphragm. She had always put it on in the privacy of the bathroom.

He was so happy she had seen things his way. God, he loved her; he wanted her too. Yet he could not touch her that way until she assured him what he would later say was the third time: she was protected.

For almost two months, they had the most wonderful time; it often reminded him of that first year. He was so happy. And from everything he could see, she was equally happy.

Then she told him she was pregnant! Two months to the day after that "first" time, she said she was pregnant. He was genuinely shocked. It was then she told him she had been using the rhythm method, she had not wanted to break the mood. His reply: "How in the hell can you use the rhythm method without telling me?"

She did not really have an answer, but she did apologize as long had been her custom.

He could not believe it. He asked whose baby was it. He would rather believe she had decided to get pregnant by someone else who wanted a baby rather than get pregnant for him. That must have been it! Surely she would not do that to a baby. No, he wouldn't ask her. But he loved her so much. Never had it occurred to him that she would deceive him. He knew girls sometimes did this, but here was an educated, sophisticated woman—all woman. More, she was the woman he loved, loved as he had no other.

Since she assured him that she had made an error in judging the time of the month, he accepted her apology. And then he said, "Get an abortion." A man who had tried his best to prevent his former wife Charlesetta from having an abortion had come to the point of commanding his second wife Claire to have an abortion. He could not believe he said that. But he was standing by his words. He was thinking, thinking rationally. He would not be a father again. As it was, he saw himself as a single father.

Now was her time to be shocked. This was something she had never counted on, never expected him to say. She reminded him of Charlesetta's abortion and how he had tried everything he could to prevent her from getting it. He explained that he had come to understand Charlesetta's decision. She had been right just as he was right now. The worst something that could have happened to them and their two children was the birth of a third baby. It had taken him a long time to see this, but he did see it.

When Claire knew she had lost that battle, she called for a truce. They should think about it. "There is nothing to think about," said he. Eventually she explained how although she was pro-choice, she herself could never have an abortion. For her, abortion was murdering a child.

He moved back downstairs.

She continued in her usual fashion—at least outwardly. Explaining to friends she could not possibly be as excited about

Pregnancy Two as she had been about Pregnancy One became easy. There is a big difference, she said. When a good friend wanted to know how she had convinced him to change his mind, she admitted that he hadn't really changed his mind; he still said he did not want a baby, but all was well.

Really close friends knew something was awry, but no one knew how wrong until he moved out of the house one Sunday.

Friday of the same week, she had the baby. She was in the hospital when he finally showed up to be the coach. She was soooo happy! She read this to mean that once again a baby had saved a marriage. Those who knew her could see it in her beautiful eyes. He visited her in the hospital every day.

But he did not move home when she left the hospital. He saw the other child daily, but noticeably steered clear of the baby.

He spent a lot of time thinking about the baby whom he said he could not think of as a baby. He forced—his word—himself to see the child. He even forced himself to take the two children to his apartment. He admitted he still worshipped Claire.

He revealed that what he would like to do was put baby Cierra in a sack and drop her in Puget Sound. No amount of telling him he did not mean that could change his mind.

He stayed around a few more months, and then he left the country. He always grudgingly sent his child support, rarely addressing his now second wife civilly.

Years have passed. The only something he says on the rare visits in which he sees neither child is that as soon as he thinks the children can understand he will tell them the whole story. He is living, he tells everyone, to tell the babies the whole story.

1992

Two Greeks

It was Friday. Candace was on her way to the Acropolis—again. She had been in Athens about six days, and although each day she said she would not visit the Acropolis again, she would eventually go "one more time." Because she had to get a plane ticket for her before-dawn flight Monday, she would get the plane ticket first. And because the travel agency was near the Acropolis, well, she reasoned, she could take one more look.

Standing in Constitution Square, she realized that of the eleven countries she had visited thus far, she had heard the least English in Athens and never from a woman. Candace quickly forgot about trying to read the many signs in Greek. Shakespeare's line "It's all Greek to me" takes on a distinctly concrete meaning when a person in Greece does not speak Greek. Having forgotten some of the Greek letters learned in elementary school, she laughed at her inability to spell the Greek words and went back to trying very hard to match the letters on the sign with the letters on the map.

"You are an American?" said a Greek with a mere hint of an accent. (She knew this man was Greek. The streets were full of men who looked a lot like the Greek sculptures she had been seeing in books since college days.) She was extremely happy to hear someone speak English.

"Yes," she responded cheerfully.

"You'll never find what you're looking for. That map is not like American maps. It doesn't go north-south, and unimportant streets aren't on it. What are you looking for?"

Candace, ignoring her sister's admonishment not to speak to strangers, gave him the address and name of the travel agency.

He did not know exactly where it was, but said he was going in that direction and would show her. His English was a welcome sound, the best she had heard in a long time, so Candace did not hesitate to ask him to pronounce the names of some of her favorite Greek characters—Oedipus, Odysseus, Achilles, Antigone, Iphigenia. He laughed at her pronunciations but said some were very good or at least satisfactory. He was surprised that she knew so much Greek literature.

His name is Constantine. He had worked in New York for six years and loved "the States," was going back as soon as he could. The two of them walked along the street exchanging information strangers often give each other: occupation, hometown, marital status, hobbies.

After a leisurely paced walk of about twenty minutes of talking, they arrived at the address. And since it would be at least two hours before she could see someone—the city was in the midst of the siesta—he suggested that Candace let him show her the nearby Parliament Gardens. Quickly but carefully surmising the situation, she assented. It was early afternoon; the streets were full of people; he assured her that she would love the sights. By now she was accustomed to meeting "foreigners" and loved listening to their questions and comments about the United States.

So off they strolled talking about movies. She saw a sign for *Deerhunter*. He had not seen the movie and wondered why it was called such. Although Candace rarely saw new releases while they were still "new," Robert DeNiro and Meryl Streep had gotten her to the theater. Candace's explanation of the title made him sure he wanted to see the film. Unintentionally, she was still being the teacher, but she was the student too. And she loved what she was learning!

Part of Constantine's reason for providing all kinds of information rested on his knowing she was a teacher. By now the two were chatting like old friends. They finally completed the tour, and he suggested that they sit on a nearby park bench. She reluctantly agreed—large, old trees and shrubbery surrounded this part of the park. Telling herself that they had talked over an hour now and had actually had a very good conversation, she decided she was safe despite the seclusion. Even so, she could now hear at least two of her sisters saying, "Be careful," especially the one who made Candace promise not to talk to strangers. Candace refused to try to explain that everyone on this trip would be a stranger. She still had more than an hour's wait before going to the travel agency.

The conversation rolled along smoothly.

After about fifteen minutes, he very casually said, "Now we can go to my room."

"Huh?"

"We can go to my room now," he repeated.

"No, I don't want to go to your room."

"But I want you. I want to make love to you."

Candace was not quite sure how the conversation got there. "Flabbergasted" is the most appropriate word for her reaction. Absolutely nothing she had said or done, at least knowingly, should have given him the impression that she wanted to go to his room or make love!

"Oh, you're accustomed to American men," he said in the voice of someone certain he knew what he was talking about. "They ask you to go to their rooms to listen to music, but they really want you to go to their rooms to make love. They aren't straightforward. We Greek men see a woman we want, we tell her. We get to the point."

As if she felt the need to defend American me, Candace said, "Some American men are like that, but not all of them. But I do not want to go to your room for any reason!"

"Why?"

"I don't know you. I'm not interested in having sex with you!"

"But I want you!"

"I don't want you. And I told you I'm married!" She thought this would make him understand.

"So? Because you are married—that is no reason for you to do without sex while you are away from home."

More flabbergasted than before, she remained seated, belittling herself for continuing the conversation but not knowing exactly what to do. Before she could think further, Constantine, with the biggest smile, crooned, "You'll come with me."

"No, I won't," she replied emphatically.

With a puzzled look on his face he said, "Your eyes do not say you are a cold woman. They say you are very warm. Now come to my room."

For some reason Candace was not afraid, but she was looking for an escape route and preparing to run if necessary although this man did not look as if he would harm her. He simply would not believe she had no intention of having sex with him.

She got up and walked away, hoping and praying she had read his demeanor correctly and he would not harm her. In that now very unwelcome accent, he whispered, "You're the first colored to turn me down!"

Despite the anger, she took this time to smile and replied, "I know many coloreds who would turn you down."

Now sad that what had been a very pleasant experience had been spoiled by his lust and simultaneously disgusted with herself for having trusted him, she kept walking, leaving him sitting on the bench.

She spent time wondering what she had done, if anything, to make him think she was ready to have a sexual encounter with him. She had thoroughly enjoyed talking to him, and the pleasure probably showed. But there was no reason for him to think she wanted to make love to him.

This was not the first time a Greek had approached her about sex. A man would speak; she would speak. No one ever appeared to be a threat. But she was annoyed that the men extended the invitation. This man had talked to her, had talked to her almost two hours. Sex had never been a subject in the discussion. There had been no warning. Of course, guidebooks sometimes warn women about traveling alone because there are places where a lone woman is understood to be a woman looking for a man, for sex. Preferring to trust her judgement, Candace had not thought too much about the conclusion in those books. Now, after traveling alone almost two weeks, she recalled what she had read but would not bring herself to say "Greek men…" She reminded herself to be more careful.

On the following Sunday Candace was coming from the Acropolis for what would definitely be the last time—she had gotten her ticket and was leaving Athens. She had one last site to visit: Kerameikos, formerly Ceramicus, an ancient Greek cemetery where many ceramic items had been found alongside the remains in the graves. But before Candace returned to the hotel, she wanted to eat. After all, she was cold and wet from the steady downpour. A brief time out of the rain and hot food to eat would be fine.

She saw a restaurant which looked inviting. Spaghetti and pizza weren't what she had planned to eat, but the rain and tiredness convinced her otherwise. After what seemed like forever, she was told by a polite waiter that spaghetti was not served on Sundays. As much as she did not want pizza, she wanted to look for another restaurant even less. Pizza she ordered.

As Candace got settled, a male customer who was at least fifty-five, possibly sixty, came to her table. "Are you an American?" Tired as she was, she looked up and smiled, happy to know there are Greeks who recognize a black American. "Are you enjoying Athens?"

"Oh, very much so."

"Please join my nephew and me?"

"Thank you very much, but I would rather not."

"All right. Enjoy your visit."

After what seemed like an hour, the pizza came. It did not look as good as she had hoped, but she was still tired, hungry, wet, and cold. Just as she lifted a slice of pizza to her mouth, the older gentleman returned: "I know you said you did not want company, but I hate to see people eat alone, especially a foreigner in my country."

After two more no's from her and three more pleadings from him, Candace agreed to eat with them.

On occasion the incident with Constantine crossed her mind, but she reasoned that because this man was much older than she was, and his nephew, probably forty, was present, she could relax. The nephew spoke but then said nothing else. Perhaps English was to him what Greek was to her, Candace concluded.

The older gentleman proudly revealed that his brother lives in Boston, that he himself had visited Boston several times and loved the U. S. He's a lawyer. He wanted to know what Candace did, what she had seen. He was proud that she knew so much about Greek literature, especially the dramas. Another interesting conversation was happening. She was warm; the pizza wasn't so bad. After about twenty minutes, the nephew left. She really felt comfortable now. The conversation got livelier. She was feeling very good.

After revealing that she was en route to Kerameikos, the Greek asked if she wanted company. Candace hesitated—not long, but long enough for him to notice. "Why are you hesitating?"

"Oh, nothing," said she.

"No, tell me why."

"No, it's silly."

"Oh, please tell me. We've had such a great conversation."

Still rather unsure about whether to tell, she calmly told him about the incident with Constantine. He listened attentively. His eyes and face said he was interested, but she could not clearly decide what the expression on his face meant. But he did seem very interested in hearing the whole story. Finally, she told the tale.

"Are you saying nothing can happen?"

With a weird sense of knowing exactly what that look meant, Candace said, "Yes, I am."

But, Candace, I've talked to you. You are a very intelligent woman. And intelligent people know we cannot predict the future."

Clearly disgusted, Candace replied, "I can."

Standing up now, the gentleman replied, "So you prefer to spend your time with the dead rather than the living. Goodbye!"

He rushed from the restaurant.

Candace sat there not quite sure whether she should laugh at his cleverness or cry at her stupidity. She had thought he was so safe! Wrong again.

At least she was dry and full and had learned more about Greece and more than she wanted to learn about another Greek. She left the restaurant determined to visit the dead.

As she was looking at the Athens map again, she heard her name.

"Candace! Candace!" This is Athens she thought. Who in Athens knows her? She turned around to see Constantine wearing the brightest of smiles.

"You're still trying to read that map? Where do you want to go? I am locked out of my apartment. I'll show you."

Index

About the Author

Georgia Stewart McDade, a Louisiana native who has lived in Seattle more than half her life, loves reading and writing. Earning a Bachelor of Arts from Southern University, Master of Arts from Atlanta University, and Ph. D. from University of Washington, the English major spent more than thirty years teaching at Tacoma Community College but also found time to teach at Seattle Community College, Seattle University, the University of Washington, Lakeside School, Renton Technical College, and Zion Preparatory Academy. As a charter member of the African-American Writers' Alliance (AAWA), McDade began reading her stories in public in 1991. For a number of years she has written poems inspired by art at such sites as Gallery 110, Seattle Art Museum, Columbia City Gallery, and Onyx Fine Arts Collective. For several years she wrote for Pacific Newspapers, especially the *South District Journal.* The prolific writer has edited several books and has works in AAWA anthologies *I Wonder as I Wander*, *Gifted Voices*, *Words? Words! Words*, and *Threads.* Her books include *Travel Tips for Dream Trips* (1988), questions and answers about her six-month, solo trip around the world; collections of poetry *Outside the Cave* (2009), *Outside the Cave II* (2012), and *Outside the Cave III* (2015); and numerous essays, stories, and poems. Among her several writing projects are the journals kept during her travels, two biographies, and an examination of the works of Jessie Fauset.

CPSIA information can be obtained
at www.ICGtesting.com
Printed in the USA
BVHW041553051121
620877BV00005B/19

9 780982 187227